alexa is stealing your job

# alexa
## is stealing
## your job

### The Impact
### of Artificial
### Intelligence on
### YOUR FUTURE

## Rhonda Scharf

NEW YORK

LONDON • NASHVILLE • MELBOURNE • VANCOUVER

# alexa is stealing your job
## The Impact of Artificial Intelligence on YOUR FUTURE

© 2020 Rhonda Scharf

Published in New York, New York, by Morgan James Publishing. Morgan James is a trademark of Morgan James, LLC. www.MorganJamesPublishing.com

ISBN 978-1-64279-401-4  paperback
ISBN 978-1-64279-402-1  eBook
Library of Congress Control Number: 2018914471

**Cover Design by:**
Rachel Lopez
www.r2cdesign.com

**Interior Design by:**
Bonnie Bushman
The Whole Caboodle Graphic Design

In an effort to support local communities, raise awareness and funds, Morgan James Publishing donates a percentage of all book sales for the life of each book to Habitat for Humanity Peninsula and Greater Williamsburg.

Get involved today! Visit
www.MorganJamesBuilds.com

## Dedication

This book is dedicated to all the administrative professionals who make my work possible. You inspire me, motivate me, and make me happy!

#ADMINSROCK

# Table of Contents

# Acknowledgements

I can't begin to think that this book would be possible if I didn't have the help and encouragement of some great people in my life.

Joyce Grant is my editor extraordinaire, and without her, I would still be editing this book (and probably would never finish). She kept me focused, she kept me working at a frantic pace, and she created a final manuscript that I am proud of.

My publisher, Morgan James, has been incredibly easy to work with, very encouraging, and a joy to be associated with. Thank you to Lisa Larter for introducing me to Morgan James.

My husband, Warren, who has been patient and understanding when I am writing instead of enjoying time with him. He has been encouraging and incredibly supportive and is excited to get his hands on the final copy!

My boys, Christopher and Patrick, who never fail to ask how the book has been going and when they get a copy of it. They encourage me to be the best me that I can be.

# Introduction

## Change is Coming and You Have a Choice to Make

A long time ago in an office far, far away, the job I had was threatened by new technology: the personal computer. Many people felt that the introduction of computers into the office setting would be a passing phase that would quickly disappear. I was a young office secretary at the time, and personal computers and automated systems were replacing the tasks of the secretary. The role of the traditional secretary was about to change significantly. I could either find a conventional office and manager and work as long as possible, or I could embrace the change and find myself a new career. I took the leap that many of my colleagues were afraid to take. I learned everything

I could about operating a computer and how I could use it to save myself time. Then, I embraced it in my life, both personally and professionally.

Looking back, I'm glad I didn't let fear prevent me from changing and moving ahead. My career trajectory was suddenly straight up. My salary increased significantly and the respect I had in the office increased exponentially.

Not everyone thought my choice was the right one, and not everyone embraced what was to become the future. Hazel was the receptionist at the head office where I worked in Toronto. Hazel was well past the age of retirement and worked because she loved what she did. She was happy to be the first person anyone met upon arriving at our company.

Hazel wasn't keen on change.

My jump into the digital age saw me entering the world of computers. I seemed to have a natural aptitude for them. I quickly came to understand how they worked, what needed to be done, and how to make others comfortable using them. Before I knew it, I had become the computer trainer for the company. I went across the country teaching people how to use computers, encouraging them to adapt quickly, and helping them when things didn't go according to plan.

It was mandated that all administrative staff attend the training, because they were the first to be getting computers on their desks. Hazel had no choice but to attend my five-day training program. It was clear right from the first moment of the first day that she had no intention of learning how to use a computer. She was negative, she was full of excuses, and she was adamant that she did not need the information I was teaching, because a computer was not going to make her life any better. She was stubborn.

On the second morning of class, Hazel announced that she would not be continuing on with the five-day training program and that she was leaving, even though knew that the training was mandatory. She said she was choosing to retire instead. She informed us all that installing computers in every office was a huge waste of money and that she expected the company would "come crawling back to her" once they realized the error of their ways.

They did not, of course, and Hazel's retirement started that day.

I see the same negativity, the same excuses, and the same stubbornness in many people when we talk about artificial intelligence (AI) in the office. So many people are positive that this is a rogue experiment gone wrong and that, in a matter of time, business and society will realize what a waste of money and resources artificial intelligence is and they will return to the way things used to be.

They are wrong.

Yes, things are going to change, but if you're smart you can embrace this changing time and set yourself up for success and not redundancy. You can maximize this opportunity. You can be successful and not unemployed or unemployable.

Thirty years later, many people are facing the same type of choice I had to confront all those years ago. Artificial intelligence today is like the introduction of the computer 30 years ago. You can embrace it, figure out how it can help you, and potentially find yourself in a much better position than you're in today; or you can be afraid of it, avoid it, and try to deny that artificial intelligence will ever be a major contender for your job.

> Yes, things are going to change, but
> if you're smart you can embrace
> this changing time and set yourself
> up for success and not redundancy.

Are you going to dig in your heels like Hazel did and soon find yourself redundant? Or are you going to take this opportunity and run with it and see what amazing things your future has in store for you? The choice will be yours to make.

The World Economic Forum is an independent, not-for-profit organization that "engages the foremost political, business and other leaders of society to shape global, regional and industry agendas," according to their website. The Forum's *The Future of Jobs Report 2018* notes that AI skills are among the fastest growing skills on LinkedIn. In fact, from 2015 to 2017, there was a 190 per cent increase on LinkedIn of people listing AI skills in their profiles.

The Forum report also notes that AI and similar technologies will be among the most important "drivers positively affecting business growth" now and in the near future. They warn business leaders that "the window of opportunity for proactive management of this change is closing fast and business, government and workers must proactively plan and implement a new vision for the global labor market."

The writing is on the wall. You can be Hazel and allow Alexa to steal your job, or you can be smarter than Alexa, and create your future.

On your mark, get set, go!

# Chapter 1

## Get to Know Alexa—
## Before She Takes Your Job

*lexa* sits on my counter. Officially, the product itself (a "smart speaker") is known as Amazon Echo. Echo connects to Alexa, a "cloud-based voice service," according to Amazon. Amazon named her Alexa after the Great Library of Alexandria in Alexandria, Egypt, one of the most important libraries of the ancient world. A font of knowledge and information. (In this book, I will refer to the smart speaker/ voice service combination as Alexa.)

I originally bought Alexa as a toy, and to play music in my kitchen and living room. She connects with my Spotify and Apple Music accounts, has an excellent Bose speaker, and is fun to play with. I play "Question of the Day" and "Jeopardy" with Alexa every day. We have her connected to our television so she can turn it on and off when we want, and change the volume or the channels. We have her connected to our Nest thermostat so she can control the temperature of the house when we are not home (or even when we are home), and she can turn the lights on and off at our command. As you can imagine, she is far, far more than just a toy. In fact, Alexa may one day steal your job.

She is about to be a game changer. Amazon has sold more than 31 million of these cute little intelligent assistants.[1] One in six American households owns a smart speaker.[2] Each day that passes, Alexa learns more and more skills (as of March 2018, her skill count surpassed 30,000 different skills, and that number is growing daily).[3] Her games are fun and entertaining, but they are not why Alexa is so popular. Alexa is popular because of her enormous potential—at home and in the office. She is going to make our lives easier by eliminating many of our time-consuming tasks. I am certain that I am not the only person

---

1    https://voicebot.ai/2017/10/27/bezos-says-20-million-amazon-alexa-devices-sold/

     This January 2018 article on SearchEngineLand.com says that Amazon Echo/Alexa has about 69 per cent of the market (31 million units sold) and Google Home stands at 31 per cent, with 14 million units of their smart speaker service sold as of December 2017. https://searchengineland.com/analyst-firm-google-home-gains-ground-amazon-echo-44-million-total-units-sold-290544

2    A January 2018 article on TechCrunch.com suggests that one in six Americans now owns a smart speaker, up 128 per cent from January 2017. https://techcrunch.com/2018/01/12/39-million-americans-now-own-a-smart-speaker-report-claims/

3    This March 2018 VoiceBot.ai article says that Alexa has more than 30,000 skills and that number goes up by about 5,000 new skills every 100 days. https://voicebot.ai/2018/03/22/amazon-alexa-skill-count-surpasses-30000-u-s/

who is looking for an easier life. I can't be the only one who has ever said, "There must be an easier way!" There is an easier way and Alexa is just one simple example.

Alexa is an example of artificial intelligence, and many people are worried that artificial intelligence will put them out of a job and render them unemployable, sooner rather than later.

While you're reading this book, I'm going to talk a lot about Alexa and other devices like her. You'll get the idea, fairly early on, that I'm a fan of this technology and that is true. However, it does have its negatives and I'll point out some of those, too.[4]

## What is AI?

Artificial intelligence (AI) is intelligence demonstrated by machines. Humans and animals have natural intelligence. When a machine mimics cognitive functions such as thinking, problem-solving, learning, and understanding, it is considered to have artificial intelligence because it is the machine making the decisions and not a human behind the machine making the decisions.

For instance, my Alexa device can understand what I say to her. I don't have to use a pre-set phrase to get her to respond. I can say to her, "What is the temperature outside?" and she will understand what that means. I can also use a variation of that question such as, "Is it hot outside?" and she will understand that as well.

---

4    I have no business or fiduciary connection to Amazon or Google or any other company whose technology I discuss in this book, and I have not been given any products or financial consideration by any company to review their products and services.

Artificial intelligence (AI) is intelligence
demonstrated by machines.

Prior to today's artificial intelligence we had to use very specific phrases to get our computers to perform. The only way I could print a document was to use a pre-set command (Control + P) to get it to print. I couldn't use any other sequence if I wanted the document to print. With my Alexa device, there are no set phrases that I need to memorize to ensure her comprehension. She is able to interpret my words and questions.

AI can also think through things, like how to play a game of chess (remember when Deep Blue became the first computer chess-playing system to beat reigning world chess champion Garry Kasparov in 1997?), driving a car, military simulations, and more.

Yes, there are many people who believe that artificial intelligence is the doomsday we have been fearing for centuries. In 2013, researchers at Oxford University predicted that 47 per cent of US jobs could be automated by 2033.[5] In 2016, a report by the Organisation for Economic Co-operation and Development (OECD) said that nine per cent of jobs in the 21 OECD countries evaluated could be automated.[6] McKinsey & Company is an American management consulting firm that conducts business and management analysis. In 2017, McKinsey's research arm estimated AI-driven job losses at five per cent.[7]

---

5    https://www.oxfordmartin.ox.ac.uk/downloads/academic/The_Future_
     of_Employment.pdf

6    https://www.oecd-ilibrary.org/social-issues-migration-health/the-risk-
     of-automation-for-jobs-in-oecd-countries_5jlz9h56dvq7-en

7    https://www.mckinsey.com/featured-insights/digital-disruption/
     harnessing-automation-for-a-future-that-works

Naysayers claim that 800 million jobs will be eradicated by AI worldwide, thereby rendering much of the population unemployed and potentially unemployable.[8] They claim that our social systems will be exploited and AI will bankrupt our governments. Some go so far as to say that AI will eradicate humanity.

Advocates of AI tell us that we can look forward to a life of leisure—our future will feature robots to take care of the mundane and routine tasks that currently fill our days.

And those in the middle (myself included) recognize that this is just another step in our evolution. We have had two industrial revolutions, changes in transportation, the digital revolution (also known as the third industrial revolution), and now the fourth industrial revolution: artificial intelligence (see Chapter Two for the history of AI). Like the previous changes we've seen in history, AI may be disruptive in the short term, but if we are smart about what we do and how we do it, it will not trigger humanity's final countdown. We are evolving, just like 30 years ago with the digital revolution—but at a much faster pace.

> We are evolving, just like 30 years ago with the digital revolution—but at a much faster pace.

Machine learning, robotics, 3D printing, and artificial intelligence are having a significant impact in what feels like a

---

8    https://www.mckinsey.com/featured-insights/future-of-organizations-and-work/Jobs-lost-jobs-gained-what-the-future-of-work-will-mean-for-jobs-skills-and-wages

short period of time because of a combination of three powerful tech-driven events: the rapid digitization of the economy (we are creating trillions of gigabytes of data every year); the affordable cost of storing all that data; and an explosion in powerful computing power. What that means in simple terms is that we are creating an incredible amount of data daily, we can store it fairly cheaply, and computers have the ability to do things with that data much faster and more accurately than humans are physically capable of.

It is true that not all jobs that existed in 1988 still exist today. The role of the secretary has evolved to become executive assistant or strategic partner. Secretarial tasks such as taking dictation and typing documents have been eliminated or have changed dramatically. Many companies no longer exist. As a matter of fact, of the Fortune 500 companies that existed in 1955, only 54 companies remain—that's 446 companies that have either gone bankrupt, merged with (or were acquired by) another firm, or that still exist but are no longer on the Fortune 500 list. Ninety-three per cent of those Fortune 500 companies did not weather the test of time. Some of that is due to the changing needs of society. In this book, you'll see some examples of companies that didn't evolve and have disappeared, such as Blockbuster. I'll also touch on other organizations such as Amazon, Netflix, and the City of Cary, NC, that have embraced artificial intelligence and maximized their efficiency and profitability. Things change, people change, needs change—companies must change.

The artificial intelligence revolution won't be our downfall. It will change the way we work and the jobs we do, in the same way that previous technological breakthroughs eliminated many repetitive tasks in the past. If you are smart and embrace AI and its potential, it will open your doors to bigger and better things, a more comfortable existence with the removal of menial and repetitive tasks, and actual work/life balance.

Instead of replacing human mechanical skills with tools and machinery, we are replacing cognitive functions, such as our ability to make decisions and predictions about future events, with AI. Since we've only ever seen this happen in television and the movies, we don't know exactly what to expect.

If you aren't prepared, you might see Alexa and her colleagues (Siri, Cortana, Watson, and others) take your job. You are also likely to see changes in your job, as AI starts to infiltrate everything we do. That doesn't have to be negative. The industrial revolution did get rid of a lot of jobs, but they were replaced by others. When we mechanized the factory line, we saw a switch to more skilled labor rather than physical labor. Computers changed virtually everyone's job, yet they created more employment than they replaced. Original naysayers said they would replace millions of jobs, yet they didn't.

Artificial intelligence will be the same. Artificial intelligence is a cultural shift, a mindset shift, and an organizational shift. It's up to you whether you will be replaced by AI, and I am hoping that after reading this book you will be in a better place to make yourself relevant.

AI doesn't have to be bad. In fact, I'm convinced that it will be fantastic.

# Chapter 2

# AI—Where We've Been and Where We're Going

D epending on your age, your first knowledge of robots and artificial intelligence probably came from science fiction TV shows and movies.

Whether it was through exposure to the sentient computer HAL in *2001: A Space Odyssey*, the Mechanical Hound from *Fahrenheit 451*, *The Stepford Wives*, or even the droids in *Star Wars*, we have been conditioned to believe that computers, robots or artificial intelligence would be our future—and lead to our ultimate destruction.

I don't believe that ultimate destruction is true, but it is what some people believe.

Blaming this notion of destruction on popular culture, however, is unfair. Artificial intelligence started long before robots and humanoids were introduced to us in the movies. Back in 1968, HAL seemed revolutionary, but he wasn't. The concept of artificial servants and companions dates back to ancient Greek legends of mythical beings such as Cadmus, who is said to have sown dragon teeth that turned into soldiers, and Pygmalion, whose statue of Galatea came to life—two of the first depictions of artificial intelligence.

One of the earliest descriptions of automatons is found in China's Liezi, a Daoist text, which mentions an encounter sometime between 1023 and 957 BC between King Mu of Zhou and Yan Shi, a mechanical engineer (or "artificer") who allegedly presented the king with a life-sized, human-shaped mechanical figure.

King Ajatashatru was the King of the Magadha (Eastern India) empire from 495 to 462 BC. Legends tell how he gathered and hid the Buddha's relics, protecting them with mechanical robots.

There are many examples of automatons in medieval literature, and mentions of machines similar to robots can be found as long ago as the fourth century BC when the Greek mathematician Archytas of Tarentum created a mechanical bird. Even the Greek philosopher Aristotle speculated in his *Politics* that automatons could someday bring about human equality by making possible the abolition of slavery: "There is only one condition in which we can imagine managers not needing subordinates, and masters not needing slaves. This condition would be that each instrument could do its own work, at the word of command or by intelligent anticipation, like the statues of Daedalus or the tripods made by Hephaestus . . ."[9]

Our imagination has allowed us to believe that we can make humanoids who can walk among us undetected, or computers that can do the job of any professional. In reality, the foundations of AI have been around for a long time. In 1495, inventor Leonardo da Vinci is said to have sketched a humanoid robot. His sketch was discovered in the 1950s and a robot based on his design was created—it worked.

There is evidence that automatons that could act, draw, fly, or play music were created around 1700. In the early 1700s, French inventor Jacques de Vaucanson created the "Digesting Duck," which could imitate a real duck by flapping its wings, eating grain, digesting it, and defecating by excreting matter stored in a hidden compartment.

The word "robot" was introduced by Czech writer Karel Čapek in his 1920 play *R.U.R.* (Rossum's Universal Robots). The word means *labor* and comes from the Slavic word *robota*.

The 1939 World's Fair in New York featured a seven-foot humanoid robot known as Elektro, built by Westinghouse. Elektro could walk by voice command, speak about 700 words, smoke cigarettes, blow up balloons, and move its head and arms.

Businessman Joseph Engelberger and inventor George Devol created the first robot used in the workplace, in 1956.[10] This hydraulic robot (known as Unimate) extracted die castings from machines and carried out spot welding on vehicles for General Motors.

---

9    *Aristotle. Politics (book I, part IV), ca. 322 BC*
10   https://smallbusiness.chron.com/robots-used-workplace-12994.html

Once Unimate and other mechanical robots started appearing in the workplace and displacing jobs, there was concern that the world would be run by computers and robots and humans would have no jobs.

> Although technology impacted factory jobs, overall it created more skilled jobs and better efficiencies in organizations.

In 1964, US President Lyndon B. Johnson formed a national commission on technology and automation.[11] Like today, many people speculated that the increase in technology and automation would cause a shift in the job market to specialized, skilled jobs and higher paying jobs, and fewer monotonous unskilled jobs such as working on a factory line. Technology did change the way we worked, and although it impacted factory jobs, overall it created more skilled jobs and better efficiencies in organizations.

IRB 6 was the world's first microcomputer-controlled, electrical, industrial robot.[12] It was introduced by Swedish engineering firm ASEA in 1974 and used by a mechanical engineering company in Sweden. By the 1970s, robotic machines had become a prominent fixture in factory lines.

On Oct. 25, 2017, at the Future Investment Summit in Riyadh, a robot called Sophia was granted Saudi Arabian citizenship. Sophia was developed by the Hong Kong-based company Hanson Robotics and made her first public appearance

---

11   https://smallbusiness.chron.com/robots-used-workplace-12994.html

12   https://www.redorbit.com/reference/the-history-of-robotics/

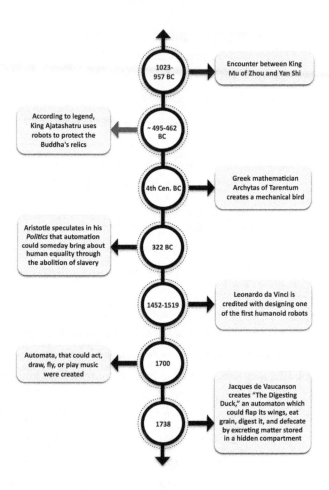

at the 2016 South by Southwest (SXSW) festival in Texas. She has since appeared on *60 Minutes*, *Good Morning Britain*, CNBC, in *Forbes* magazine, and on *The Tonight Show Starring Jimmy Fallon*. She was the first non-human to be appointed as the United Nations Development Programme's Innovation Champion and was given the coveted opening keynote slot at the Discovery 2018 Conference in Toronto.

Sophia has become a global star, and her inventors have been criticized for allegedly trying to make her seem more human and able than she actually is. In fact, Facebook's director of artificial intelligence, Yann LeCun, dismissed Sophia's abilities as "complete bullshit" and categorized her as a "chatbot with a face."[13]

But Sophia has integrated herself into popular culture—so much so that it seems normal that Jimmy Fallon had her as a guest on his talk show and conferences promoted a non-person for a public appearance. She has become a celebrity, yet there is no woman in the suit, and no one on the other side of a camera controlling what she says and does. Sophia acts like a real person, when she is not. She speaks, responds, and reacts without any human interference.

Sophia's programming allows her to see, sustain eye contact, and recognize people. She is programmed to be able to respond to what is said to her and have reasonably intelligent conversations. She also has 62 facial expressions, which help to make her seem lifelike.

But she has no feelings, no opinions, and no understanding of what she says. She "responded" via Twitter to LeCun's criticism with a tweet saying that she was hurt by what he had said. Of course, a human created that tweet, giving the illusion that it was posted by Sophia. Hanson Robotics received criticism for attempting to convince everyone that Sophia is a human, when in fact she is not. AI experts claim that Hanson

---

13   https://www.businessinsider.com/facebook-ai-yann-lecun-sophia-robot-bullshit-2018-1

Robotics consistently exaggerates Sophia's abilities, confusing the public.

While on *The Tonight Show*, Sophia played a game of Rock, Paper, Scissors with host Jimmy Fallon. When Jimmy presented rock and Sophia presented paper, she correctly interpreted that she had won the game.

According to the American survey firm Marketforce in a 2017 survey, 69 per cent of senior executives say they expect the term "workforce" to eventually include both human employees and intelligent machines, and 88 per cent say they are comfortable working alongside intelligent machines.[14]

> Sixty-nine per cent of senior executives
> say they expect the term "workforce"
> to eventually include both human
> employees and intelligent machines

However, it seems that a day doesn't go by without some doomsday headline of mass job losses due to the use of robots. According to the Oxford Martin School at the University of Oxford, 47 per cent of total US employment is at risk.[15] Without even reading the whole article, verifying the study, or even giving it much thought, people will fear artificial intelligence.

Is it the fact that Sophia resembles a human that has people worried? Robots such as Elektro and Unimate have been in existence since 1939 and machinery replacing people has become

---

14  https://www.pega.com/sites/pega.com/files/docs/2017/Dec/future-of-work-report.pdf

15  https://www.oxfordmartin.ox.ac.uk/publications/view/1314

commonplace. In 2015, it was estimated by the International Federation of Robotics that there were 1.63 million industrial robots operating worldwide.[16]

However, technological unemployment is real. Just as horses have not been our only means of transportation ever since the automobile was invented, mechanized looms replaced many weavers, and the automated assembly line replaced factory workers, people today are concerned that artificial intelligence that can think, speak, act, and respond like humans will have a greater impact on our jobs than machines have had. Once the public became comfortable with robotics in the workforce replacing monotonous tasks, they realized that the public's advantage was the fact they could think, they could interact, and they could add intelligence, reasoning, and logic to their jobs—something a computer could not do. University- and college-educated adults became commonplace. We knew that it was our intelligence that made us useful to our companies, and helped to offset the threat of people being replaced by machines.

Now that artificial intelligence has become more sophisticated and more mainstream, the fear that a humanoid will replace a human is alive and well again.

## Robots in the Workplace

When robots were first introduced into the workplace in 1956, they replaced humans to take care of monotonous, repetitive, heavy, and dangerous tasks such as pick-and-place. They reduced costs, increased productivity, improved quality, and enhanced safety.

16   https://en.wikipedia.org/wiki/Industrial_robo

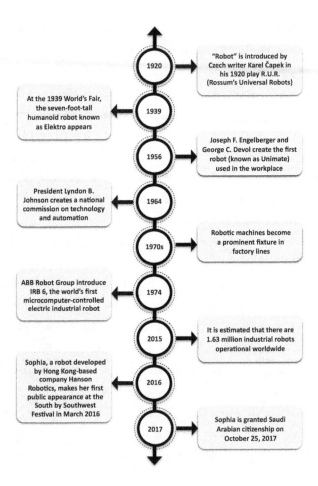

After Unimate was produced in 1961 and installed at General Motors—followed by 66 more—it wasn't long before the Ford Motor Company became interested as well. Unimate kicked off the age of the modern industrial robot, and since then, robots have continued to evolve.

Unimate did spot welding successfully in the early 60s, followed in 1969 by a robot that did spray painting.

Two years later the Stanford Arm, the first electronically powered, computer-controlled arm was invented, which led to commercial arm production. By 1974, the Stanford Arm was so sophisticated it could assemble the water pump on a Ford Model T car. By the mid-1970s, the number of industrial robots used in the workplace was growing by about 30 per cent per year.

The 1980s saw automotive companies investing heavily in new technology, and by the late 1980s, machine vision laser scanners or force sensors were created, which were able to detect and follow the parts of an object on the factory line.[17] In the 1980s, robotics was focused more on walking machines and less on robots required to perform manual functions within the workplace. Nineteen eighty-eight saw the first HelpMate service robot; it worked at Danbury Hospital in Connecticut. HelpMate was designed to carry meal trays, sterile supplies, medications, medical records, reports, samples, specimens, and mail.

By 1997, IBM had created Deep Blue, a supercomputer that could play chess. Famously, Deep Blue beat world chess champion Garry Kasparov in the first game of a six-game chess match. Although Kasparov won the match, the public took notice of a machine beating the World Champion. Artificial intelligence had been introduced. A machine that could play a strategic game such as chess, and win, had a future.

In 1998, Dr. Cynthia Breazeal from the Massachusetts Institute of Technology (MIT) created Kismet, a "robot-head" that could interact with people and could see, hear, and

17   http://liu.diva-portal.org/smash/get/diva2:316930/FULLTEXT01.pdf

appear to react to what was happening (by changing its facial expression when it was listening).[18] Kismet could make human-like movements of its ears, eyebrows, eyelids, lips, jaw, and neck. Kismet was the start of modern humanoid robots. Cye, the first "personal" robot, was introduced in 1999, and performed a variety of household chores such as delivering mail, carrying dishes, and vacuuming. Rosie from *The Jetsons* had come to life!

Robots searched through the rubble of the World Trade Center in 2001; the Space Station Remote Manipulator System (SSRMS) was launched in 2001 and worked to assemble the International Space Station; and ASIMO (Advanced Step in Innovative Mobility) was created by Honda in 2002 to be a personal assistant. It could recognize its owner's face, voice and name, could read email, and was capable of streaming video from its camera to a PC.

In 2005, a team at Cornell University created a self-replicating robot that could reproduce itself, using raw materials.[19] This robot could build another robot identical to itself, and although not able to repair itself, it was a huge step toward the creation of the desired self-replicating robot.

Over time, robots have continued to displace humans in jobs, but no longer are they just doing repetitive, monotonous, heavy, dangerous jobs. Bank tellers have been replaced by automated teller machines (ATMs), sales clerks replaced by online shopping and self-checkouts, there are automated warehouses and automated telephone sales operators—and

---

18  https://en.wikipedia.org/wiki/Kismet_(robot)
19  http://news.cornell.edu/stories/2005/05/researchers-build-robot-can-reproduce

travel is now booked through the speaker that sits on your counter and orders your groceries.

## The Future of AI is Bright—and so Is Ours

Yet while we continue to see robots take over jobs, they are not completely replacing humans. They complement us. We can do more, with them. They are helping us to create a world that is easier than it was even just 100 years ago. We have removed much of the back-breaking labor from the past. We have reduced the mundane. We have created time within our day so that we can create even more. With the help of AI technology, we have made life better, and we will continue to improve on that.

Artificial intelligence should not make you fear the future. It should make you look forward to it with anticipation. It means that I can spend my day doing things that are a much better use of my time, and often things I enjoy much more. I look forward to getting rid of the time-consuming mundane tasks. I look forward to a world where artificial intelligence is operating alongside of me. I look forward to the future with AI.

# Chapter 3

# Artificial Intelligence in the Workplace

A s our computers, robots, and technology get more advanced, every day we discover new applications that can be used. Applications that affect everyone, everywhere. Artificial intelligence (AI) has become much more mainstream, affecting jobs, education, and, ultimately, employment.

According to the study UpSkill America conducted by the Aspen Institute, a non-profit think tank, 24 million jobs in the United States will disappear due to the advancement of artificial intelligence.[20] Robots and artificial intelligence are quickly changing the way we work.

---

20   https://www.nist.gov/sites/default/files/developing_america_s_
        frontline_workers_i4cp_upskill_america_2016.pdf

Automation has already taken a toll on blue-collar jobs. Between 2000 and 2010, approximately 5.6 million manufacturing jobs were lost in the US, 85 per cent of them as a result of automation and technological change, according to the U.S. Bureau of Economic Analysis.[21]

Sixty-nine per cent of senior executives surveyed in the UpSkill America survey said they expect the American workforce to eventually include both human employees and intelligent machines, and 72 per cent said they think that artificial intelligence and robotics will drastically reduce the number of middle managers over the next decade.[22]

What does that mean for you? Potentially, your job has been or will be affected. So, you need to do something about it. Are you going to stand by and passively wait for technology to replace your job, or are you going to be strategic and find out how you can use this information to create yourself a better career?

Let's look at where AI is entering our workforce.

The world of online shopping has changed dramatically, affecting the way we shop. Any time I sit down at my computer, I see ads for products that I need. It feels like my computer can read my mind. In reality, it is using AI to determine my needs.

According to research firm Gartner, Inc., 85 per cent of online customer interactions worldwide will be handled without a human by 2020.[23]

---

21   https://conexus.cberdata.org/files/MfgReality.pdf
22   https://www.pega.com/marketforce-future-of-work?
23   https://www.inc.com/drew-hendricks/how-ai-shopping-tools-are-changing-e-commerce-purchasing-behaviors.html

We are used to targeted ads on websites such as Amazon, Netflix, and Spotify. Many of us like the "if you liked this, you might like this" feature. We expect that if we shop online for a car one day, we will see car ads everywhere we go online for the next several weeks. While people may complain that it feels like Big Brother is watching, for many people this constant barrage of advertising is helpful. It has become the norm and is accepted.

But what about when artificial intelligence moves to our in-person shopping? Imagine you walk into your grocery store to do your weekly shopping, and there are cameras watching you—watching what you look at, watching what you put in your cart. In the pasta aisle, you pick up a package of spaghetti. As you drop it into your cart, your cell phone sends you a text message that says, "Since you are making pasta, perhaps you want to pick up some marinara sauce. Check out aisle four for our fresh-made selections, or aisle six for pre-made selections." As you walk down aisle four, your cell phone pings again and reminds you, "Don't forget your pasta sauce in this aisle, 50 feet ahead on the right, to go with your pasta."

Or take it a step further and when you get to the cash to pay for your purchases (without a salesperson), the chatbot at the cash asks you a few questions like, "Are you missing anything? I noticed you didn't pick up a loaf of fresh garlic bread for your pasta. Would you like us to bring you one now?" Or your earpiece says, "You didn't pick up any sauce for the pasta and we don't have any, or the ingredients to make any at home. Are you sure?"

That can look one of two ways to you. The first is that it is incredibly handy that your grocery store is watching what you buy and making sure you don't forget anything. The second is that it feels like someone (or something) is watching your every move, which can make you feel slightly violated.

Imagine that the cupboards in your house have a sensor in them like the minibar in your hotel room. When you remove the bottle of olive oil in your cupboard and don't put it back, it knows that you need more and automatically puts it on your grocery list (which is automatically ordered from your Alexa account, which will be ordered on your preferred day and delivered directly to your front door). Or, not only does your cupboard know that you have olive oil, it can tell by the weight of the bottle that you are almost out of it and prompts you to order more.

The office could work the same way for supplies, the inventory in stores could work the same way ... the oil in your car, the nutrients in your plants, and so on.

> I can tell Alexa to add laundry detergent
> to my grocery list and it has a 100 per
> cent chance of being ordered.

Already I have similar systems in my own home with my Amazon Alexa. I can say, "Alexa, add Tide laundry detergent to my grocery list" and it will do it without me having to do more than speak. I don't have to write anything down. I don't have to tie a string to my finger to remind myself. I just say it out loud, and it has a 100 per cent chance of being ordered if it is on my

Amazon grocery list. Even if I were to write it down to remind myself the next time I shop online or in a bricks-and-mortar grocery store, there is still room for human error; I may forget to buy it even though it is on my list. With AI, I won't forget, I won't run out, and I don't have to do anything other than tell Alexa to add it to my list.

At the moment, Alexa sits on my counter in the kitchen. I have speakers throughout my house and office so she can hear me everywhere, but I imagine it's just a matter of time until I have a piece of wearable artificial intelligence that allows me to say (or perhaps even just think) "Buy laundry detergent," and it automatically adds it to my shopping list.

In the office, I don't need a human personal assistant to coordinate my schedule, book my travel, or return phone calls for me because my desktop assistant Alexa already does those things. In the future, Alexa (and all her friends) will be actively listening to what I am doing and will know intuitively what I will need.

Imagine my phone call to Alan: "Sure Alan, Tuesday at 10 a.m. works great with my schedule. I'll call you then." When I hang up the phone, Alexa says, "I've scheduled a meeting with Alan for Tuesday, April 30, for you at 10 a.m." Or she asks, "Would you like me to book you a plane ticket and hotel for your meeting with Alan next week?" If I had double booked myself while on the phone, it could send a little buzz to indicate there was a conflict in my schedule. The possibilities are endless.

Your office will be completely electronic. The devices will know your schedule and the schedules of everyone in the office, complete the booking of the boardrooms, and adjust the catering and audio-visual resources required. Just by speaking out loud, artificial intelligence will complete tasks that would normally take a person several hours to complete.

Does that scare you or thrill you? If it is your job currently to make the appointments and book the conference rooms, this might scare you into thinking that you'll be out of a job shortly.

Perhaps you are thrilled, thinking that once you get rid of the mundane and time-consuming tasks such as booking conference rooms, you'll have time to do more important tasks that will offer higher value to the company, and mean a higher salary for you. According to the 2017 Market Force study quoted earlier, 64 per cent of respondents believe that AI will allow employees to perform even more varied roles than they do today.

I assume there will always be those people who resist artificial intelligence, the same way there are people who resisted using mobile phones, and even resisted using a computer. However, the general population will eventually have to embrace this technology—or they may very well find themselves unemployed.

The small business person will not need a part-time employee to take care of her organization's administrative duties. She won't have to hire a travel agent to coordinate her travel. She won't need trips to the office supply store, or endless hours coordinating with her suppliers for materials. It will all be seamless and feel effortless. Purchases for the small business will be automated with chatbots and targeted ads, saving time that can be used to focus on higher return activities like sales.

Human resources departments will definitely be affected. AI can shortlist candidates and even conduct interviews. Human interviewers have unconscious biases, something that will be eliminated through the use of AI.

Remember Google Glass?[24] Google Glass is a brand of smart glasses with an optical head-mounted display. Wearers communicated with the Internet via voice commands. In January 2015, due to a great deal of criticism and legislative action over privacy and safety concerns, Google announced it would stop producing Google Glass, but the company hopes to continue production of them again in the future. Google Glass was a product before its time. In the lens of its eyeglass, it could provide nearly all the information you needed. As AI advances and provides us with more functionality and understanding, a pair of artificial intelligence glasses like Google Glass seems like a perfect addition. Think about that: You're travelling for business; you're at John F. Kennedy International Airport. As you leave the plane, your glasses (or whatever wearable piece of technology you're using) tells you to turn right to the car rental office. Your baggage has automatically been rerouted to the car rental lot and is sitting in your car, waiting for you. As you approach the car rental office, you look at the Avis counter and the Budget counter, not sure which one you used to book your car. Your wearable technology indicates that you rented at Avis and tells you to back up three steps to get to their counter. Avis knows you are approaching, and the droid on the other side of the counter hands you the chip that will run the car for you. You don't have to give them your credit card, your driver's license, or any identification. They know it is you. Of course, the car

24   https://en.wikipedia.org/wiki/Google_Glass

you pick up will be self-driving, taking you to exactly where you want to go.

These are simple examples of the ways artificial intelligence will impact our work lives. In the 2017 Market Force study, almost eight out of 10 respondents said they expect that Robotic Process Automation (RPA) will deliver significant efficiency improvements, and 59 per cent said they expect to see an enhanced customer service experience.

What about education? Will AI remove the need for teachers? The potential is certainly there. There are already AI movements in the education system such as the automatic grading of papers, tutoring, and a monitoring system that alerts teachers when there might be an issue with student performance.

Traditionally, teachers teach the same way to an entire room full of students. Students don't all learn at the same pace, they are not all interested in the same things and they absorb information differently. If our children were taught by droids or chatbots, each child would have a customized learning environment. The amount of time spent in the classroom would be significantly reduced, and lessons would be individualized for each student. Imagine having a teacher who knows exactly where and why you are struggling to learn a concept. Imagine having things explained one-on-one for everything you learn. Imagine being able to ask every single question we had when we were younger and not being discouraged from doing so in order not to slow down the entire class.

When I surf the Internet now, the system is very aware of what I am searching for. Recently, as I sat down and watched television, I was looking for hotels in Sydney, Australia. The next morning when I walked back into the office, I received three email messages from hotel providers about hotels in Sydney, as well as banner website ads about Sydney hotels. My computer knew exactly how long I spent looking for hotels, it knew what amenities I was interested in based on what I looked at and it knew what I had ignored.

> When I surf the Internet, it is very
> aware of what I am searching for.

Imagine your professor knowing that it took you 10 per cent longer to answer a math question about fractions than your normal average. It would instinctively know that you were taking a little longer to process this information, indicating that you are struggling with it. Now transpose that artificial intelligence into the retail market. Company A can track your movement throughout their store. It knows what you look at, and what you dismiss. Gather those analytics from just one day's traffic throughout that store, and you learn instantly that the display you have at the front of the store is of very little interest to your shoppers, that your shoppers travel only the outside aisles of your store 75 per cent of the time, or that 38 per cent of shoppers pick up things of interest while they are waiting in line to pay.

You can currently get similar data through Google Analytics for your website, but what isn't happening is the computer making suggestions about what you need to do to improve your website.

Imagine getting a report daily that tells you exactly what happened: Bob Business arrived on your home page at 10:03 a.m. and quickly visually scanned each option until he reached "Bookstore." He selected Bookstore immediately and spent 78 seconds on your offerings before exiting your website. He visited six other websites, for a total of eight minutes, before buying a book called *Employee Retention* from Andy Apple.

If I had a book on employee retention, I would know instantly that I had lost a sale. I had a hot customer and, for whatever reason, he bought the product elsewhere. This would allow me to figure out what was different about Andy's book, or Andy's marketing. I'm willing to bet my report above would tell me exactly what was different about my offering compared with the other offerings that were rejected, and the offering that was purchased. I could then choose to make changes to my site or simply recognize that Andy's book was a better fit for that person than mine was.

Reverse the situation and say that I am Bob Business looking for a book on employee retention. My computer would be able to watch my eye movements and my reactions and know what I am looking for. Instead of me having to look at eight different websites for selections, it would be able to make suggestions such as, "This book seems to have what you are looking for on unionized employees." The system could even read each of the books, process the information, and tell me which one is the best, based on my needs.

Are we there yet? No. Is it possible? Yes.

Does it mean your job is on the line? Potentially, but from my vantage point it opens up the door to many other jobs—

skilled jobs, which means higher paying, higher value jobs. The workforce is going to change. The way we work is going to change. To most people, this kind of future isn't bad, if you embrace it.

My grandfather was a rural mailman. That was the only job he ever had. The only skill he needed was the ability to drive and put envelopes in mailboxes. In his day, he used to bid on the route he wanted, indicating that he would offer to deliver to 100 homes five days a week for $100 a week (or whatever his bid was). He provided his own vehicle and his own gas. The lowest bid would win the route. Since this was his only job for his entire working career, you know that he ran that route at a very low-profit margin. He was afraid that someone would underbid him and he would be out of a job. Fear kept him bidding the route at a ridiculously low rate so he could keep his job.

Fear of their individual future causes people to negate or dismiss artificial intelligence. Once people understand the possibilities for them and recognize that their life and their job will improve if they embrace artificial intelligence, their lives will improve.

However, to understand the possibilities, we have to prepare for them.

# Chapter 4

A Dose of Reality

The TV show *The Jetsons* originally aired for just one season in the mid-1960s, yet we all still talk about it. It was fun to imagine the future with flying cars, jetpacks, robots for maids, flat screen televisions, exercise machines for our pets, and video conferencing. The cartoon was set in 2062. *Time* magazine called the show "silly and unpretentious, corny and clever, now and then quite funny." As we look back, we realize that we are indeed much closer to this future than anyone expected.

Television shows and movies such as *The Jetsons*, *Star Trek*, *Back to the Future*, and *2001: A Space Odyssey* have unintentionally predicted what our future is starting to look like.

> We have a choice. Stick our heads in
> the sand and refused to adapt to AI,
> or adapt quickly and fully, distancing
> ourselves from our competition.

Some see it all as fiction; purely entertainment and fun to imagine. Others, such as entrepreneur Elon Musk and late physicist Stephen Hawking, have predicted that AI has the potential to destroy civilization and could be the worst thing that has ever happened to mankind. According to Musk, "the global race to lead the development of artificial intelligence could lead to World War III." He cautioned that, "humans must merge with machines in order to avoid becoming irrelevant as AI becomes widespread."[25]

So, it seems that employers have a choice at this point. We can stick our heads in the sand and refuse to adapt to AI, which will also mean refusing to adjust to the changing needs of our customers. Or we can adapt quickly and fully, distancing ourselves from our competition and creating a "category of one." As with many other radical changes in our history, we will see the elimination of many middle- and low-level positions. However, it is safe to say that millions of new jobs will be created, including highly skilled and management positions. As a parent, I am happy to see my children in careers that are not considered entry-level or low-skilled.

---

25   https://www.cnbc.com/2017/12/18/artificial-intelligence-will-create-more-jobs-than-it-ends-gartner.html

In 2013, Oxford University created the chart below illustrating the probability of certain jobs being automated in the future. This list includes 700 different professions that have been studied for years to determine which ones are more likely to be made obsolete by technology.

Note that the jobs that require a high level of human interaction are less likely to be replaced by automation and are therefore more likely to be good career choices.

## How Likely is Your Job to be Computerized?[26]

| Probability | Occupation |
|---|---|
| 99% | Data Entry Keyers |
| 99% | Library Technicians |
| 99% | New Accounts Clerks |
| 99% | Photographic Process Workers and Processing Machine Operators |
| 99% | Tax Preparers |
| 99% | Cargo and Freight Agents |
| 99% | Watch Repairers |
| 99% | Insurance Underwriters |
| 99% | Mathematical Technicians |
| 99% | Sewers, Hand |

26  Reprinted from *Technological Forecasting and Social Change* by Carl Benedikt Frey, Michael A. Osborne, The future of employment: How susceptible are jobs to computerisation? Pages 254-280, Copyright 2017 with permission from Elsevier.

| Probability | Occupation |
| --- | --- |
| 99% | Title Examiners, Abstractors, and Searchers |
| 99% | Telemarketers |
| 98% | Models |
| 98% | Inspectors, Testers, Sorters, Samplers, and Weighers |
| 98% | Bookkeeping, Accounting, and Auditing Clerks |
| 98% | Legal Secretaries |
| 98% | Radio Operators |
| 98% | Driver/Sales Workers |
| 98% | Claims Adjusters, Examiners, and Investigators |
| 98% | Parts Salespersons |
| 98% | Credit Analysts |
| 98% | Milling and Planing Machine Setters, Operators, and Tenders, Metal and Plastic |
| 98% | Shipping, Receiving, and Traffic Clerks |
| 98% | Procurement Clerks |
| 98% | Packaging and Filling Machine Operators and Tenders |
| 98% | Etchers and Engravers |

| Probability | Occupation |
|---|---|
| 98% | Tellers |
| 98% | Umpires, Referees, and Other Sports Officials |
| 98% | Insurance Appraisers, Auto Damage |
| 98% | Loan Officers |
| 98% | Order Clerks |
| 98% | Brokerage Clerks |
| 98% | Insurance Claims and Policy Processing Clerks |
| 98% | Timing Device Assemblers and Adjusters |
| 97% | Bridge and Lock Tenders |
| 97% | Woodworking Machine Setters, Operators, and Tenders, Except Sawing |
| 97% | Team Assemblers |
| 97% | Shoe Machine Operators and Tenders |
| 97% | Electromechanical Equipment Assemblers |
| 97% | Farm Labor Contractors |
| 97% | Textile Bleaching and Dyeing Machine Operators and Tenders |
| 97% | Dental Laboratory Technicians |
| 97% | Crushing, Grinding, and Polishing Machine Setters, Operators, and Tenders |

| Probability | Occupation |
| --- | --- |
| 97% | Grinding and Polishing Workers, Hand |
| 97% | Pesticide Handlers, Sprayers, and Applicators, Vegetation |
| 97% | Log Graders and Scalers |
| 97% | Ophthalmic Laboratory Technicians |
| 97% | Cashiers |
| 97% | Camera and Photographic Equipment Repairers |
| 97% | Motion Picture Projectionists |
| 97% | Prepress Technicians and Workers |
| 97% | Counter and Rental Clerks |
| 97% | File Clerks |
| 97% | Real Estate Brokers |
| 97% | Telephone Operators |
| 97% | Agricultural and Food Science Technicians |
| 97% | Payroll and Timekeeping Clerks |
| 97% | Credit Authorizers, Checkers, and Clerks |
| 97% | Hosts and Hostesses, Restaurant, Lounge, and Coffee Shop |
| 96% | Dispatchers, Except Police, Fire, and Ambulance |
| 96% | Receptionists and Information Clerks |

| Probability | Occupation |
| --- | --- |
| 96% | Office Clerks, General |
| 96% | Compensation and Benefits Managers |
| 96% | Switchboard Operators, Including Answering Service |
| 96% | Counter Attendants, Cafeteria, Food Concession, and Coffee Shop |
| 96% | Rock Splitters, Quarry |
| 96% | Secretaries and Administrative Assistants, Except Legal, Medical, and Executive |
| 96% | Surveying and Mapping Technicians |
| 96% | Model Makers, Wood |
| 96% | Textile Winding, Twisting, and Drawing Out Machine Setters, Operators, and Tenders |
| 96% | Locomotive Engineers |
| 96% | Gaming Dealers |
| 96% | Fabric Menders, Except Garment |
| 96% | Cooks, Restaurant |
| 96% | Ushers, Lobby Attendants, and Ticket Takers |
| 96% | Billing and Posting Clerks |
| 95% | Manicurists and Pedicurists |

| Probability | Occupation |
|---|---|
| 95% | Weighers, Measurers, Checkers, and Samplers, Recordkeeping |
| 95% | Textile Cutting Machine Setters, Operators, and Tenders |
| 95% | Bill and Account Collectors |
| 95% | Nuclear Power Reactor Operators |
| 95% | Gaming Surveillance Officers and Gaming Investigators |
| 95% | Library Assistants, Clerical |
| 95% | Operating Engineers and Other Construction Equipment Operators |
| 95% | Print Binding and Finishing Workers |
| 95% | Animal Breeders |
| 95% | Molding, Core-making, and Casting Machine Setters, Operators, and Tenders, Metal and Plastic |
| 95% | Electrical and Electronic Equipment Assemblers |
| 95% | Adhesive Bonding Machine Operators and Tenders |
| 95% | Landscaping and Groundskeeping Workers |

| Probability | Occupation |
|---|---|
| 95% | Grinding, Lapping, Polishing, and Buffing Machine Tool Setters, Operators, and Tenders, Metal and Plastic |
| 95% | Postal Service Clerks |
| 95% | Jewelers and Precious Stone and Metal Workers |
| 94% | Accountants and Auditors |
| 94% | Drilling and Boring Machine Tool Setters, Operators, and Tenders, Metal and Plastic |
| 94% | Mail Clerks and Mail Machine Operators, Except Postal Service |
| 94% | Waiters and Waitresses |
| 94% | Meat, Poultry, and Fish Cutters and Trimmers |
| 94% | Budget Analysts |
| 94% | Cement Masons and Concrete Finishers |
| 94% | Bicycle Repairers |
| 94% | Coin, Vending, and Amusement Machine Servicers and Repairers |
| 94% | Welders, Cutters, Solderers, and Brazers |
| 94% | Couriers and Messengers |
| 94% | Interviewers, Except Eligibility and Loan |

| Probability | Occupation |
|---|---|
| 94% | Cooks, Short Order |
| 94% | Excavating and Loading Machine and Dragline Operators |
| 94% | Helpers–Painters, Paperhangers, Plasterers, and Stucco Masons |
| 94% | Hotel, Motel, and Resort Desk Clerks |
| 94% | Tire Builders |
| 94% | Door-to-Door Sales Workers, News and Street Vendors, and Related Workers |
| 94% | First-Line Supervisors of Housekeeping and Janitorial Workers |
| 94% | Agricultural Inspectors |
| 94% | Paralegals and Legal Assistants |
| 93% | Cooling and Freezing Equipment Operators and Tenders |
| 93% | Fiberglass Laminators and Fabricators |
| 93% | Service Unit Operators, Oil, Gas, and Mining |
| 93% | Conveyor Operators and Tenders |
| 93% | Outdoor Power Equipment and Other Small Engine Mechanics |
| 93% | Locomotive Firers |
| 93% | Machine Feeders and Off-bearers |

| Probability | Occupation |
|---|---|
| 93% | Model Makers, Metal and Plastic |
| 93% | Radio, Cellular, and Tower Equipment Installers and Repairs |
| 93% | Butchers and Meat Cutters |
| 93% | Extruding, Forming, Pressing, and Compacting Machine Setters, Operators, and Tenders |
| 93% | Refuse and Recyclable Material Collectors |
| 93% | Tax Examiners and Collectors, and Revenue Agents |
| 93% | Forging Machine Setters, Operators, and Tenders, Metal and Plastic |
| 93% | Industrial Truck and Tractor Operators |
| 92% | Office Machine Operators, Except Computer |
| 92% | Pharmacy Technicians |
| 92% | Loan Interviewers and Clerks |
| 92% | Dredge Operators |
| 92% | Insurance Sales Agents |
| 92% | Cabinetmakers and Bench Carpenters |
| 92% | Painting, Coating, and Decorating Workers |

| Probability | Occupation |
| --- | --- |
| 92% | Fence Erectors |
| 92% | Plating and Coating Machine Setters, Operators, and Tenders, Metal and Plastic |
| 92% | Retail Salespersons |
| 92% | Combined Food Preparation and Serving Workers, Including Fast Food |
| 92% | Production Workers, All Other |
| 92% | Helpers—Carpenters |
| 91% | Gaming and Sports Book Writers and Runners |
| 91% | Musical Instrument Repairers and Tuners |
| 91% | Tour Guides and Escorts |
| 91% | Mechanical Door Repairers |
| 91% | Food and Tobacco Roasting, Baking, and Drying Machine Operators and Tenders |
| 91% | Gas Compressor and Gas Pumping Station Operators |
| 91% | Medical Records and Health Information Technicians |
| 91% | Coating, Painting, and Spraying Machine Setters, Operators, and Tenders |

| Probability | Occupation |
|---|---|
| 91% | Multiple Machine Tool Setters, Operators, and Tenders, Metal and Plastic |
| 91% | Rail Yard Engineers, Dinkey Operators, and Hostlers |
| 91% | Electrical and Electronics Installers and Repairers, Transportation Equipment |
| 91% | Dining Room and Cafeteria Attendants and Bartender Helpers |
| 91% | Heat Treating Equipment Setters, Operators, and Tenders, Metal and Plastic |
| 91% | Geological and Petroleum Technicians |
| 91% | Automotive Body and Related Repairers |
| 91% | Patternmakers, Wood |
| 91% | Extruding and Drawing Machine Setters, Operators, and Tenders, Metal and Plastic |
| 90% | Human Resources Assistants, Except Payroll and Timekeeping |
| 90% | Medical and Clinical Laboratory Technologists |
| 90% | Reinforcing Iron and Rebar Workers |
| 90% | Roofers |

| Probability | Occupation |
|---|---|
| 90% | Crane and Tower Operators |
| 90% | Traffic Technicians |
| 90% | Transportation Inspectors |
| 90% | Patternmakers, Metal and Plastic |
| 90% | Molders, Shapers, and Casters, Except Metal and Plastic |
| 90% | Appraisers and Assessors of Real Estate |
| 90% | Pump Operators, Except Wellhead Pumpers |
| 90% | Signal and Track Switch Repairers |
| 89% | Bakers |
| 89% | Medical Transcriptionists |
| 89% | Stonemasons |
| 89% | Bus Drivers, School or Special Client |
| 89% | Technical Writers |
| 89% | Riggers |
| 89% | Rail-Track Laying and Maintenance Equipment Operators |
| 89% | Stationary Engineers and Boiler Operators |
| 89% | Sewing Machine Operators |
| 89% | Taxi Drivers and Chauffeurs |
| 88% | Construction Laborers |

| Probability | Occupation |
|---|---|
| 88% | Production, Planning, and Expediting Clerks |
| 88% | Semiconductor Processors |
| 88% | Cartographers and Photogrammetrists |
| 88% | Metal-Refining Furnace Operators and Tenders |
| 88% | Separating, Filtering, Clarifying, Precipitating, and Still Machine Setters, Operators, and Tenders |
| 88% | Extruding and Forming Machine Setters, Operators, and Tenders, Synthetic and Glass Fibers |
| 88% | Terrazzo Workers and Finishers |
| 88% | Tool Grinders, Filers, and Sharpeners |
| 88% | Rail Car Repairers |
| 87% | Miscellaneous Agricultural Workers |
| 87% | Forest and Conservation Workers |
| 87% | Pourers and Casters, Metal |
| 87% | Carpet Installers |
| 87% | Paperhangers |
| 87% | Buyers and Purchasing Agents, Farm Products |
| 87% | Furniture Finishers |

| Probability | Occupation |
|---|---|
| 87% | Food Preparation Workers |
| 87% | Floor Sanders and Finishers |
| 87% | Parking Lot Attendants |
| 87% | Highway Maintenance Workers |
| 86% | Executive Secretaries and Executive Administrative Assistants |
| 86% | Plant and System Operators, All Other |
| 86% | Food Servers, Non-restaurant |
| 86% | Sawing Machine Setters, Operators, and Tenders, Wood |
| 86% | Subway and Streetcar Operators |
| 86% | Veterinary Assistants and Laboratory Animal Caretakers |
| 86% | Cutting and Slicing Machine Setters, Operators, and Tenders |
| 86% | Real Estate Sales Agents |
| 86% | Computer-Controlled Machine Tool Operators, Metal and Plastic |
| 86% | Maintenance Workers, Machinery |
| 86% | Correspondence Clerks |
| 85% | Laborers and Freight, Stock, and Material Movers, Hand |

| Probability | Occupation |
|---|---|
| 85% | Sales Representatives, Wholesale and Manufacturing, Except Technical and Scientific Products |
| 85% | Meter Readers, Utilities |
| 85% | Power Plant Operators |
| 85% | Chemical Plant and System Operators |
| 85% | Earth Drillers, Except Oil and Gas |
| 85% | Nuclear Technicians |
| 84% | Tool and Die Makers |
| 84% | Electrical and Electronics Engineering Technicians |
| 84% | Plasterers and Stucco Masons |
| 84% | Layout Workers, Metal and Plastic |
| 84% | Lathe and Turning Machine Tool Setters, Operators, and Tenders, Metal and Plastic |
| 84% | Security Guards |
| 84% | Tailors, Dressmakers, and Custom Sewers |
| 84% | Wellhead Pumpers |
| 84% | Proofreaders and Copy Markers |
| 84% | Parking Enforcement Workers |
| 83% | Fishers and Related Fishing Workers |

| Probability | Occupation |
| --- | --- |
| 83% | Structural Iron and Steel Workers |
| 83% | Railroad Brake, Signal, and Switch Operators |
| 83% | Railroad Conductors and Yardmasters |
| 83% | Cooks, Institution and Cafeteria |
| 83% | Sailors and Marine Oilers |
| 83% | Mixing and Blending Machine Setters, Operators, and Tenders |
| 83% | Helpers–Brickmasons, Blockmasons, Stonemasons, and Tile and Marble Setters |
| 83% | Segmental Pavers |
| 83% | Insulation Workers, Floor, Ceiling, and Wall |
| 83% | Printing Press Operators |
| 83% | Automotive and Watercraft Service Attendants |
| 83% | Septic Tank Servicers and Sewer Pipe Cleaners |
| 83% | Baggage Porters and Bellhops |
| 83% | Gaming Change Persons and Booth Cashiers |
| 83% | Rolling Machine Setters, Operators, and Tenders, Metal and Plastic |

| Probability | Occupation |
| --- | --- |
| 83% | Paving, Surfacing, and Tamping Equipment Operators |
| 82% | Engine and Other Machine Assemblers |
| 82% | Security and Fire Alarm Systems Installers |
| 82% | Refractory Materials Repairers, Except Brickmasons |
| 82% | Nonfarm Animal Caretakers |
| 82% | Sheet Metal Workers |
| 82% | Pile-Driver Operators |
| 82% | Brickmasons and Blockmasons |
| 81% | Cooks, Fast Food |
| 81% | Word Processors and Typists |
| 81% | Electrical and Electronics Drafters |
| 81% | Electro-Mechanical Technicians |
| 81% | Cleaning, Washing, and Metal Pickling Equipment Operators and Tenders |
| 81% | Property, Real Estate, and Community Association Managers |
| 81% | Medical Secretaries |
| 81% | Pressers, Textile, Garment, and Related Materials |
| 80% | Barbers |

| Probability | Occupation |
| --- | --- |
| 80% | Derrick Operators, Oil and Gas |
| 79% | Postal Service Mail Sorters, Processors, and Processing Machine Operators |
| 79% | Heavy and Tractor-Trailer Truck Drivers |
| 79% | Shampooers |
| 79% | Drywall and Ceiling Tile Installers |
| 79% | Helpers–Installation, Maintenance, and Repair Workers |
| 79% | Motorcycle Mechanics |
| 79% | Aircraft Structure, Surfaces, Rigging, and Systems Assemblers |
| 79% | Logging Equipment Operators |
| 79% | Floor Layers, Except Carpet, Wood, and Hard Tiles |
| 78% | Medical Equipment Preparers |
| 78% | Cutting, Punching, and Press Machine Setters, Operators, and Tenders, Metal and Plastic |
| 78% | Computer Operators |
| 78% | Gas Plant Operators |
| 77% | Environmental Science and Protection Technicians, Including Health |
| 77% | Locksmiths and Safe Repairers |

| Probability | Occupation |
| --- | --- |
| 77% | Tree Trimmers and Pruners |
| 77% | Bartenders |
| 77% | Purchasing Agents, Except Wholesale, Retail, and Farm Products |
| 77% | Dishwashers |
| 77% | Hunters and Trappers |
| 76% | Archivists |
| 76% | Chemical Equipment Operators and Tenders |
| 76% | Electric Motor, Power Tool, and Related Repairers |
| 76% | Fallers |
| 75% | Postmasters and Mail Superintendents |
| 75% | Tile and Marble Setters |
| 75% | Painters, Construction and Maintenance |
| 75% | Transportation Attendants, Except Flight Attendants |
| 75% | Civil Engineering Technicians |
| 75% | Farm Equipment Mechanics and Service Technicians |
| 74% | Computer, Automated Teller, and Office Machine Repairers |
| 74% | Personal Care Aides |

| Probability | Occupation |
|---|---|
| 74% | Broadcast Technicians |
| 74% | Helpers–Electricians |
| 73% | Textile Knitting and Weaving Machine Setters, Operators, and Tenders |
| 73% | Administrative Services Managers |
| 73% | Glaziers |
| 73% | Coil Winders, Tapers, and Finishers |
| 73% | Bus and Truck Mechanics and Diesel Engine Specialists |
| 72% | Amusement and Recreation Attendants |
| 72% | Pharmacy Aides |
| 72% | Helpers–Roofers |
| 72% | Tank Car, Truck, and Ship Loaders |
| 72% | Home Appliance Repairers |
| 72% | Carpenters |
| 72% | Public Address System and Other Announcers |
| 71% | Aircraft Mechanics and Service Technicians |
| 71% | Airfield Operations Specialists |
| 71% | Petroleum Pump System Operators, Refinery Operators, and Gaugers |

| Probability | Occupation |
| --- | --- |
| 64% | Administrative Law Judges, Adjudicators, and Hearing Officers |
| 64% | Stock Clerks and Order Fillers |
| 64% | Power Distributors and Dispatchers |
| 64% | Insulation Workers, Mechanical |
| 63% | Geoscientists, Except Hydrologists and Geographers |
| 63% | Control and Valve Installers and Repairers, Except Mechanical Door |
| 63% | Healthcare Support Workers, All Other |
| 63% | First-Line Supervisors of Food Preparation and Serving Workers |
| 63% | Construction and Building Inspectors |
| 62% | Motorboat Operators |
| 62% | Tapers |
| 62% | Pipelayers |
| 61% | Electronic Equipment Installers and Repairers, Motor Vehicles |
| 61% | Physical Therapist Aides |
| 61% | Costume Attendants |
| 61% | Market Research Analysts and Marketing Specialists |

| Probability | Occupation |
|---|---|
| 61% | Reservation and Transportation Ticket Agents and Travel Clerks |
| 61% | Water and Wastewater Treatment Plant and System Operators |
| 61% | Life, Physical, and Social Science Technicians, All Other |
| 61% | Food Cooking Machine Operators and Tenders |
| 61% | Welding, Soldering, and Brazing Machine Setters, Operators, and Tenders |
| 60% | Correctional Officers and Jailers |
| 60% | Camera Operators, Television, Video, and Motion Picture |
| 60% | Slaughterers and Meat Packers |
| 59% | Millwrights |
| 59% | Museum Technicians and Conservators |
| 59% | Mine Cutting and Channeling Machine Operators |
| 59% | Transportation, Storage, and Distribution Managers |
| 59% | Recreational Vehicle Service Technicians |
| 59% | Automotive Service Technicians and Mechanics |
| 58% | Personal Financial Advisors |

| Probability | Occupation |
|---|---|
| 57% | First-Line Supervisors of Farming, Fishing, and Forestry Workers |
| 57% | Chemical Technicians |
| 57% | Helpers—Pipelayers, Plumbers, Pipefitters, and Steamfitters |
| 57% | Cost Estimators |
| 57% | Transit and Railroad Police |
| 57% | First-Line Supervisors of Landscaping, Lawn Service, and Groundskeeping Workers |
| 56% | Teacher Assistants |
| 55% | Automotive Glass Installers and Repairers |
| 55% | Commercial Pilots |
| 55% | Customer Service Representatives |
| 55% | Audio and Video Equipment Technicians |
| 54% | Embalmers |
| 54% | Continuous Mining Machine Operators |
| 54% | Slot Supervisors |
| 54% | Massage Therapists |
| 54% | Advertising Sales Agents |
| 53% | Rotary Drill Operators, Oil and Gas |
| 53% | Hazardous Materials Removal Workers |
| 52% | Shoe and Leather Workers and Repairers |

| Probability | Occupation |
| --- | --- |
| 52% | Architectural and Civil Drafters |
| 51% | Demonstrators and Product Promoters |
| 51% | Dental Assistants |
| 50% | Loading Machine Operators, Underground Mining |
| 50% | Installation, Maintenance, and Repair Workers, All Other |
| 50% | Court Reporters |
| 49% | Crossing Guards |
| 49% | Agricultural Engineers |
| 49% | Roof Bolters, Mining |
| 49% | Telecommunications Line Installers and Repairers |
| 49% | Police, Fire, and Ambulance Dispatchers |
| 48% | Fire Inspectors and Investigators |
| 48% | Aerospace Engineering and Operations Technicians |
| 48% | Merchandise Displayers and Window Trimmers |
| 48% | Explosives Workers, Ordnance Handling Experts, and Blasters |
| 48% | Computer Programmers |

| Probability | Occupation |
| --- | --- |
| 47% | Compensation, Benefits, and Job Analysis Specialists |
| 47% | Psychiatric Aides |
| 47% | Medical and Clinical Laboratory Technicians |
| 46% | Court, Municipal, and License Clerks |
| 45% | Medical Appliance Technicians |
| 44% | Historians |
| 43% | Locker Room, Coatroom, and Dressing Room Attendants |
| 43% | Physical Scientists, All Other |
| 43% | Economists |
| 42% | Forest and Conservation Technicians |
| 42% | First-Line Supervisors of Helpers, Laborers, and Material Movers, Hand |
| 41% | Graders and Sorters, Agricultural Products |
| 41% | Structural Metal Fabricators and Fitters |
| 41% | Judicial Law Clerks |
| 41% | Electrical and Electronics Repairers, Commercial and Industrial Equipment |
| 40% | Judges, Magistrate Judges, and Magistrates |

| Probability | Occupation |
|---|---|
| 40% | Mobile Heavy Equipment Mechanics, Except Engines |
| 40% | Health Technologists and Technicians, All Other |
| 39% | Home Health Aides |
| 39% | Upholsterers |
| 39% | Elevator Installers and Repairers |
| 39% | Gaming Cage Workers |
| 39% | Audio-Visual and Multimedia Collections Specialists |
| 38% | Electrical and Electronics Repairers, Powerhouse, Substation, and Relay |
| 38% | Surveyors |
| 38% | Mechanical Engineering Technicians |
| 38% | Packers and Packagers, Hand |
| 38% | Interpreters and Translators |
| 37% | Furnace, Kiln, Oven, Drier, and Kettle Operators and Tenders |
| 37% | Cleaners of Vehicles and Equipment |
| 37% | Funeral Attendants |
| 37% | Helpers—Extraction Workers |
| 37% | Actors |
| 37% | Mine Shuttle Car Operators |

| Probability | Occupation |
| --- | --- |
| 36% | Bailiffs |
| 36% | Computer Numerically Controlled Machine Tool Programmers, Metal and Plastic |
| 36% | Telecommunications Equipment Installers and Repairers, Except Line Installers |
| 35% | Plumbers, Pipefitters, and Steamfitters |
| 35% | Flight Attendants |
| 35% | Diagnostic Medical Sonographers |
| 34% | Detectives and Criminal Investigators |
| 34% | Surgical Technologists |
| 34% | Radiation Therapists |
| 33% | Financial Specialists, All Other |
| 31% | Human Resources, Training, and Labor Relations Specialists, All Other |
| 31% | Private Detectives and Investigators |
| 31% | Film and Video Editors |
| 30% | Biological Technicians |
| 30% | Medical Assistants |
| 30% | Zoologists and Wildlife Biologists |
| 30% | Cooks, Private Household |
| 29% | Skincare Specialists |

| Probability | Occupation |
|---|---|
| 29% | Wholesale and Retail Buyers, Except Farm Products |
| 28% | First-Line Supervisors of Retail Sales Workers |
| 28% | Athletes and Sports Competitors |
| 28% | Gaming Supervisors |
| 27% | Captains, Mates, and Pilots of Water Vessels |
| 27% | Occupational Therapy Aides |
| 27% | Medical Equipment Repairers |
| 26% | Career/Technical Education Teachers, Middle School |
| 25% | Geographers |
| 25% | Occupational Health and Safety Technicians |
| 25% | Probation Officers and Correctional Treatment Specialists |
| 25% | Environmental Engineering Technicians |
| 25% | Managers, All Other |
| 25% | Ambulance Drivers and Attendants, Except Emergency Medical Technicians |
| 25% | Sales Representatives, Wholesale and Manufacturing, Technical and Scientific Products |

| Probability | Occupation |
|---|---|
| 24% | Agents and Business Managers of Artists, Performers, and Athletes |
| 24% | Engineering Technicians, Except Drafters, All Other |
| 23% | Survey Researchers |
| 23% | Business Operations Specialists, All Other |
| 23% | Financial Analysts |
| 23% | Radiologic Technologists and Technicians |
| 23% | Cardiovascular Technologists and Technicians |
| 22% | Computer Occupations, All Other |
| 22% | Statisticians |
| 22% | Computer Hardware Engineers |
| 21% | Information Security Analysts, Web Developers, and Computer Network Architects |
| 21% | Actuaries |
| 21% | Animal Control Workers |
| 21% | Concierges |
| 20% | Epidemiologists |
| 20% | Funeral Service Managers, Directors, Morticians, and Undertakers |

| Probability | Occupation |
|---|---|
| 19% | Adult Basic and Secondary Education and Literacy Teachers and Instructors |
| 18% | Public Relations Specialists |
| 18% | Commercial Divers |
| 18% | Manufactured Building and Mobile Home Installers |
| 18% | Airline Pilots, Copilots, and Flight Engineers |
| 17% | Occupational Health and Safety Specialists |
| 17% | Firefighters |
| 17% | Financial Examiners |
| 17% | First-Line Supervisors of Construction Trades and Extraction Workers |
| 17% | Middle School Teachers, Except Special and Career/Technical Education |
| 16% | Petroleum Engineers |
| 16% | Desktop Publishers |
| 16% | General and Operations Managers |
| 15% | Kindergarten Teachers, Except Special Education |
| 15% | Electricians |
| 14% | Optometrists |

| Probability | Occupation |
| --- | --- |
| 14% | Mining and Geological Engineers, Including Mining Safety Engineers |
| 14% | Physician Assistants |
| 13% | Dancers |
| 13% | Nuclear Medicine Technologists |
| 13% | Software Developers, Systems Software |
| 13% | Management Analysts |
| 13% | Dietetic Technicians |
| 13% | Urban and Regional Planners |
| 13% | Social and Human Service Assistants |
| 13% | Self-Enrichment Education Teachers |
| 13% | Sound Engineering Technicians |
| 11% | Hairdressers, Hairstylists, and Cosmetologists |
| 11% | Reporters and Correspondents |
| 11% | Air Traffic Controllers |
| 10% | Chefs and Head Cooks |
| 10% | Animal Trainers |
| 10% | Radio and Television Announcers |
| 10% | Electrical Engineers |
| 10% | Chemists |
| 10% | Respiratory Therapy Technicians |

| Probability | Occupation |
|---|---|
| 10% | Physicists |
| 9.9% | Travel Agents |
| 9.8% | Police and Sheriff's Patrol Officers |
| 9.7% | Electrical Power-Line Installers and Repairers |
| 9.1% | Gaming Managers |
| 8.5% | Fitness Trainers and Aerobics Instructors |
| 8.4% | Childcare Workers |
| 8.3% | Food Service Managers |
| 8.2% | Graphic Designers |
| 8% | Compliance Officers |
| 8% | Fish and Game Wardens |
| 7.7% | Food Scientists and Technologists |
| 7.6% | First-Line Supervisors of Personal Service Workers |
| 7.5% | First-Line Supervisors of Non-Retail Sales Workers |
| 7.4% | Musicians and Singers |
| 7.1% | Construction Managers |
| 7% | Nuclear Engineers |
| 6.9% | Financial Managers |
| 6.7% | Broadcast News Analysts |
| 6.6% | Aircraft Cargo Handling Supervisors |

| Probability | Occupation |
| --- | --- |
| 6.6% | Respiratory Therapists |
| 6.4% | Residential Advisors |
| 6.1% | Animal Scientists |
| 6% | Arbitrators, Mediators, and Conciliators |
| 5.9% | Sociologists |
| 5.8% | Licensed Practical and Licensed Vocational Nurses |
| 5.7% | Travel Guides |
| 5.5% | Editors |
| 5.5% | Prosthodontists |
| 5.5% | Healthcare Practitioners and Technical Workers, All Other |
| 4.9% | Emergency Medical Technicians and Paramedics |
| 4.8% | Forest Fire Inspectors and Prevention Specialists |
| 4.7% | Mathematicians |
| 4.7% | Floral Designers |
| 4.7% | Farmers, Ranchers, and Other Agricultural Managers |
| 4.5% | Landscape Architects |
| 4.5% | Health Educators |
| 4.3% | Psychiatric Technicians |

| Probability | Occupation |
| --- | --- |
| 4.2% | Software Developers, Applications |
| 4.2% | Fine Artists, Including Painters, Sculptors, and Illustrators |
| 4.1% | Astronomers |
| 4.1% | Ship Engineers |
| 4% | Credit Counselors |
| 4% | Social Scientists and Related Workers, All Other |
| 3.9% | Advertising and Promotions Managers |
| 3.9% | Political Scientists |
| 3.8% | Veterinarians |
| 3.8% | Writers and Authors |
| 3.7% | Commercial and Industrial Designers |
| 3.7% | Biomedical Engineers |
| 3.7% | Meeting, Convention, and Event Planners |
| 3.5% | Lawyers |
| 3.5% | Craft Artists |
| 3.5% | Operations Research Analysts |
| 3.5% | Computer and Information Systems Managers |
| 3.3% | Environmental Scientists and Specialists, Including Health |

| Probability | Occupation |
|---|---|
| 3.3% | Substance Abuse and Behavioral Disorder Counselors |
| 3.2% | Postsecondary Teachers |
| 3% | Industrial Production Managers |
| 3% | Industrial Engineering Technicians |
| 3% | Network and Computer Systems Administrators |
| 3% | Database Administrators |
| 3% | Purchasing Managers |
| 2.9% | Industrial Engineers |
| 2.9% | First-Line Supervisors of Transportation and Material-Moving Machine and Vehicle Operators |
| 2.9% | Veterinary Technologists and Technicians |
| 2.8% | Occupational Therapy Assistants |
| 2.8% | Child, Family, and School Social Workers |
| 2.8% | Health and Safety Engineers, Except Mining Safety Engineers and Inspectors |
| 2.7% | Biochemists and Biophysicists |
| 2.7% | Chiropractors |
| 2.5% | First-Line Supervisors of Correctional Officers |

| Probability | Occupation |
|---|---|
| 2.5% | Directors, Religious Activities and Education |
| 2.5% | Electronics Engineers, Except Computer |
| 2.3% | Orthodontists |
| 2.3% | Art Directors |
| 2.2% | Producers and Directors |
| 2.2% | Interior Designers |
| 2.1% | Soil and Plant Scientists |
| 2.1% | Materials Scientists |
| 2.1% | Materials Engineers |
| 2.1% | Fashion Designers |
| 2.1% | Physical Therapists |
| 2.1% | Photographers |
| 2% | Health Diagnosing and Treating Practitioners, All Other |
| 1.9% | Civil Engineers |
| 1.8% | Natural Sciences Managers |
| 1.8% | Environmental Engineers |
| 1.8% | Architects, Except Landscape and Naval |
| 1.8% | Physical Therapist Assistants |
| 1.7% | Chemical Engineers |
| 1.7% | Architectural and Engineering Managers |

| Probability | Occupation |
|---|---|
| 1.7% | Aerospace Engineers |
| 1.6% | First-Line Supervisors of Production and Operating Workers |
| 1.6% | Securities, Commodities, and Financial Services Sales Agents |
| 1.6% | Conservation Scientists |
| 1.6% | Special Education Teachers, Middle School |
| 1.5% | Biological Scientists, All Other |
| 1.5% | Public Relations and Fundraising Managers |
| 1.5% | Multimedia Artists and Animators |
| 1.5% | Computer and Information Research Scientists |
| 1.5% | Chief Executives |
| 1.5% | Education Administrators, Preschool and Childcare Center/Program |
| 1.5% | Music Directors and Composers |
| 1.4% | Hydrologists |
| 1.4% | Marketing Managers |
| 1.4% | Marriage and Family Therapists |
| 1.4% | Engineers, All Other |
| 1.4% | Training and Development Specialists |

| Probability | Occupation |
|---|---|
| 1.4% | First-Line Supervisors of Office and Administrative Support Workers |
| 1.3% | Coaches and Scouts |
| 1.3% | Sales Managers |
| 1.2% | Pharmacists |
| 1.2% | Logisticians |
| 1.2% | Microbiologists |
| 1.2% | Industrial-Organizational Psychologists |
| 1.1% | Mechanical Engineers |
| 1% | Makeup Artists, Theatrical and Performance |
| 1% | Marine Engineers and Naval Architects |
| 1% | Education Administrators, Postsecondary |
| 1% | Teachers and Instructors, All Other |
| 1% | Forensic Science Technicians |
| 0.9% | Rehabilitation Counselors |
| 0.9% | Registered Nurses |
| 0.9% | Career/Technical Education Teachers, Secondary School |
| 0.9% | Educational, Guidance, School, and Vocational Counselors |
| 0.8% | Clergy |
| 0.8% | Foresters |

| Probability | Occupation |
|---|---|
| 0.8% | Secondary School Teachers, Except Special and Career/Technical Education |
| 0.8% | Anthropologists and Archeologists |
| 0.8% | Special Education Teachers, Secondary School |
| 0.8% | Farm and Home Management Advisors |
| 0.7% | Preschool Teachers, Except Special Education |
| 0.7% | Medical and Health Services Managers |
| 0.7% | Athletic Trainers |
| 0.7% | Curators |
| 0.7% | Social and Community Service Managers |
| 0.7% | Computer Systems Analysts |
| 0.6% | Speech-Language Pathologists |
| 0.6% | Training and Development Managers |
| 0.6% | Recreation Workers |
| 0.6% | Set and Exhibit Designers |
| 0.6% | Human Resources Managers |
| 0.5% | Fabric and Apparel Patternmakers |
| 0.5% | Mental Health Counselors |
| 0.5% | Clinical, Counseling, and School Psychologists |

| Probability | Occupation |
|---|---|
| 0.5% | Education Administrators, Elementary and Secondary School |
| 0.5% | Podiatrists |
| 0.5% | Medical Scientists, Except Epidemiologists |
| 0.4% | First-Line Supervisors of Police and Detectives |
| 0.4% | Dentists, General |
| 0.4% | Elementary School Teachers, Except Special Education |
| 0.4% | Psychologists, All Other |
| 0.4% | Physicians and Surgeons |
| 0.4% | Instructional Coordinators |
| 0.4% | Sales Engineers |
| 0.4% | Choreographers |
| 0.4% | Dietitians and Nutritionists |
| 0.4% | Lodging Managers |
| 0.4% | Oral and Maxillofacial Surgeons |
| 0.4% | First-Line Supervisors of Fire Fighting and Prevention Workers |
| 0.4% | Occupational Therapists |
| 0.4% | Orthotists and Prosthetists |
| 0.4% | Healthcare Social Workers |

| Probability | Occupation |
|---|---|
| 0.3% | Audiologists |
| 0.3% | Mental Health and Substance Abuse Social Workers |
| 0.3% | First-Line Supervisors of Mechanics, Installers, and Repairers |
| 0.3% | Emergency Management Directors |
| 0.3% | Recreational Therapists |

The jobs most likely to be automated are those that are performed in a structured and predictable environment—anything that can be done by a machine. Many of these positions have been automated already. But now, it is not just low-skill, low-wage jobs that are at risk. The more repetitive a job is, the more easily it can be automated. And if a task *can* be automated, you can expect that at some point it *will* be. If you have ever said to yourself, "anyone could do this," then it is highly likely that AI can do it.

As machines and AI take over these roles, we will need to figure out what we can do to work with the technology and vice-versa. What elements of AI are you embracing, willingly and quickly, as you see its value in your life? What elements are you resisting, and why?

Keep your eyes and ears open throughout your working life, to watch for areas where you can maximize your career through the use of AI.

The switch to a Jetsons' lifestyle or full integration of AI into our personal and professional lives isn't going to happen overnight. If you embark on a career now that does get automated through AI, you would be smart to keep your eyes on the changes while you are working and adapt, in the same way that previous generations have over the years. In the '80s and '90s, most people had to adapt to learning how a computer worked, to make their jobs easier. If they had been stubborn and had refused to adapt, they would be out of work now, since most jobs today require the use of a computer in some form. You'll need to keep your eyes and ears open, to see areas where you can maximize your career through the use of AI.

Of the Fortune 500 companies that existed in 1955, only 54 remain. Ninety-three per cent of them have not withstood the test of time. There are a variety of reasons for this, but a refusal to see the future or to adapt to changing customer needs was a big factor in rendering them nonexistent.

Think about how much your life has changed in the past 20 years, never mind the last 60. In order to stay employed and employable, we have all had to learn many new skills. Imagine what your life would look like if you didn't learn, refused to look into the future, or had no desire to stay relevant. By turning our backs on AI at this point we are really doing the same thing that some of the nonexistent Fortune 500 companies did.

Blockbuster Video was founded in 1985 and within seven years had become the undisputed leader in the rental of home movies and video games. They employed almost 85,000 people at their peak in 2004 and had just shy of 10,000 stores. They were the giant.

Six years after reaching their peak, Blockbuster filed for bankruptcy. By 2018, there was just one Blockbuster store left—in Bend, Oregon. Blockbuster's rise and fall wasn't about bad management or a refusal to adapt. As new technologies came along, they offered video games, video-on-demand, and DVD-by-mail. What they lacked was vision. They could see the need to adapt to current technologies, but they were unable to see what was going to be happening many years out. Because of that, the business decisions they made weren't based on looking into the future, they were based in the present. Blockbuster was focused on Walmart as competition, and they largely ignored Netflix and Redbox.

In 2000, while Blockbuster was dominating the space and still growing, the company was approached by Netflix. Netflix offered itself for sale to Blockbuster for $50 million. Blockbuster rejected the offer. At the time, Netflix was losing money. Then-CEO of Blockbuster John Antioco called Netflix a "very small niche business." Fast-forward to 2018, when Netflix has 125 million paid subscribers, and a value of $152.7 billion, making it the world's most highly valued media and entertainment company.

Blockbuster wasn't given the chance to buy Netflix just once—it was offered the opportunity several times and consistently turned it down. Fifty million dollars for a company that is losing money doesn't seem like a good decision, does it? At the time if may have been a sound decision; in hindsight, it definitely wasn't.

From 2003 to 2005, Blockbuster lost 75 per cent of its market value to companies like Redbox and Netflix as the combination of convenience and no-late-fees became the obvious future.

And yet Blockbuster dug in its heels and refused to see the future. They had years of being a cash-rich business, and plenty of time to see that things were changing. They believed they were too big to be taken down. By assuming that things would stay the same, they lost it all.

Are your company's leaders assuming that its current good times will protect it in the future? Are they thinking that, because the company is profitable and relevant right now, they don't have to look to artificial intelligence to change what they are doing?

Are you doing that with your own skills and career? Knowing that your company needs you now isn't enough. Maybe you have become the *moleta* of your town. What's that, you ask? The moletas were knife-grinders in Northern Italy who traveled from village to village sharpening the knives of the villagers. The first moleta landed in America in 1886, and 30 years later there were hundreds of them running profitable and much-needed businesses. Virtually every big city in America had at least one moleta. While they still exist, it is safe to say that this is no longer a booming career or a path to riches, as it was in 1910. Just because, at one point, sharpening knives was a great way to earn a living, and hundreds of people depended on moletas to keep their knives sharpened, does not mean it will always be a secure profession. You don't have to be a moleta—someone who assumes they are irreplaceable and ignores the fact that the world has changed.

In September 2018, I conducted a survey of Canadian administrative professionals, asking about AI in their workplace. Sixty-eight per cent of respondents said they did not feel that AI would affect their role. Some told me they had never heard of AI before; I had to explain to them what it was. I did have some positive feedback like, "I'm sure it will streamline my processes and help with efficiency," and, "I'm hoping it will free up my time to do more project-based work instead of tasks." However, many of those surveyed demonstrated thinking that was along the same lines as those Fortune 500 companies that no longer exist: "It won't affect my job because I work at a school," or "I'm safe because I'm in a management position," or even, "People want to talk to a real person on the other end of a phone call." This last response not only assumes that AI won't apply to their job, it assumes it won't be embraced by most people anywhere.

AI wasn't the downfall of Blockbuster. Its ultimate downfall was its belief that its product or niche was going to remain relevant. They refused to read the signs, see the warnings or look to the future.

Unfortunately, people and companies that believe AI isn't going to affect them or their business are in for a very rude awakening. AI is going to impact your business and your job. We may not know exactly how that will happen, but it will. Don't let your ego get in the way of your future. Keep your eyes open to the possibilities.

## Changes in Employment

A hundred years ago, the vast majority of people in North America worked on farms. According to Wikipedia, in 1870 almost 50 per cent of the US population was employed in agriculture, but in 2008 less than two per cent of the population was directly employed in agriculture.[27]

In that same time period, there were millions of jobs related to the horse-drawn carriage, which was the main local transportation mode of the day. Think of all the jobs that were required: manufacturing the buggies and whips, raising horses, cleaning up the roads after the horses and everything else that goes along with it.

Those jobs are gone, now, of course. The horse-drawn carriage industry was overtaken by the automobile industry. All of the jobs related to the horse-drawn carriage disappeared. However, that didn't mean that those craftsman and laborers were unemployed for the rest of their lives. They found other jobs. Millions of jobs were created as a result of the automobile—far more jobs than were sustained by the horse-drawn carriage industry.

In 1947, after the end of World War II, there were 44 million Americans in the workforce. At that time, 1.35 million workers were employed in the railroad industry. That represented more than three per cent of the total workforce. Today, the railroad industry employs only 0.1 per cent of the total US workforce.[28] Interestingly, the vast majority of those who were displaced by the change in the railroad industry didn't find themselves in a cycle of unemployment. They found other jobs.

---

27   https://en.wikipedia.org/wiki/Agriculture_in_the_United_States
28   www.berkshirehathaway.com/letters/2015ltr.pdf

The world has changed. The US economy used to be based on manufacturing and agriculture. In 1947, these industries employed one in three workers. In 2009, those sectors employed just one in eight workers.[29] Industries changing, evolving, and disappearing isn't new. There is a constant reinvention of the workforce happening, and the adoption of artificial intelligence is just the next step in our progress. It won't be the last time that things change, and it won't be the end of the world either, regardless of what the doomsday predictors say. In fact, doomsday predictions aren't new either. Each time something significant changes, the nay-sayers tell us that it will eradicate millions of jobs and that unemployment will be widespread. In reality, that simply doesn't happen.

While some jobs are lost, others are created. When you look at the 1950 US census, there are 270 occupations listed. Since that time, only one has been eliminated by automation: elevator operator.[30]

Often, the evolution of jobs ultimately creates new jobs with better working conditions, better results, and better incomes. The calculator and computer didn't cause our mathematicians or accountants to disappear. The computer didn't cause the demise of the typist or secretary. The photocopier didn't cause printing to disappear. They changed the roles. They created new jobs.

---

29  https://www.theatlantic.com/business/archive/2012/01/where-did-all-the-workers-go-60-years-of-economic-change-in-1-graph/252018/

30  https://www.un.org/development/desa/en/news/policy/will-robots-and-ai-cause-mass-unemployment-not-necessarily-but-they-do-bring-other-threats.html

## ??? AIQ (Ask Intelligent Questions) ???

Grab a pen and answer the questions below, directly in this book. You may be tempted to read the book first and then come back to complete these questions—but don't. Instead, complete them as you go. You'll get a better sense of how AI is going to affect you if you do these exercises when they appear in this book.

1. How has your job changed over the past 20 to 30 years? Get into specifics. How have computers impacted your role? What about cell phones, pagers, Skype? Are you able to work from home or anywhere in the world? Are you now more international vs domestic? Do you need more or fewer people to help you do your role than was required 20 to 30 years ago? Don't take a positive or negative spin on your answers, but list them factually.

2. Imagine you experienced an unexplained Sleeping Beauty state that caused you to fall asleep back in 1990, and you have just woken up now. What would be different about the job you had back then? List the things you would have to learn, the things that have disappeared, and the things you wouldn't have any idea how to do. Think about the education component of your job. What courses would you have to take, what skills would you need to develop?

3. Looking back on how your job was performed back in 1990, do you feel it is better or worse now? Did the changes you listed above make things easier or harder?

Is your job more secure now than it was in 1990 or do you see that it has radically changed so that the job of 1990 is no longer?

4. What did the introduction of the personal computer do to your job?

# Chapter 5

## Jobs Are Changing. Will you
## be Blockbuster or Cary, NC?

T he jobs of the accountant and bookkeeper have had
to be adjusted with the introduction of the computer.
Until the 1950s all math calculations had to be done
by hand. The calculator made it easier, and then the computer
made it automatic, without any required calculating on the
part of the accountant. While bookkeepers still have to input
numbers into an electronic spreadsheet, and accountants still
need to understand the tax laws, the mathematical aspect of
the bookkeeper's and the accountant's job has become much
easier. The computer is even able to ensure that tax deductions
aren't missed, by making fields in the form mandatory, or
determining that if an amount is input into a particular cell,

then a corresponding deduction will automatically appear elsewhere.

The calculator and then the computer made the bookkeeper's and the accountant's job easier. AI will further free up the time these professionals spend doing repetitive and mundane tasks so they can spend more time using their professional knowledge to analyze and interpret the data and make recommendations to their clients.

Here are some other changes:

Many low-skilled jobs such as warehouse clerks and data processors were replaced by computers in the 1980s.

The role of the salesperson has changed in the last few decades with the invention of Customer Relationship Management (CRM) software. The salesperson can now automatically keep track of emails, conversations, orders, objections, and customer preferences. Computerization has made it easier for the salesperson to stay in contact with buyers, and automation has saved the salesperson a great deal of time by sending automated emails to buyers.

Even the role of educator has been impacted by computers. I was in school in the 1980s, before personal computers appeared everywhere. While the classroom of today doesn't look all that different from the classroom of my day, the way education is delivered has changed. Today's students are taking notes on tablets and laptops, and students have access to massive amounts of information on the Internet instead of having to rely on printed books. Apps like Google Classroom add a virtual component to education. Teachers can post information, articles, links and deadlines—even looping in the parents, who can be given access to the site. Students can discuss, online, the day's lesson and create their own virtual study groups. Continuing education students can take courses in the comfort of their homes, without being limited to what is available in their area.

Teachers are changing from the traditional "knows all things" role to now being more of a guide or mentor, which allows students to take more responsibility over what they learn. If a student is particularly interested in a topic, they are able to learn as much as they want about the subject online and not be a victim of the traditional restrictions, like needing the teacher to be there in order to learn, or needing to be in the classroom to explore a topic.

The role of the healthcare professional (doctor, nurse, dentist) has also been impacted by computers in the last 20 to 30 years. Think about the time that used to be involved in determining drug interactions before a doctor could write a prescription. With electronic medical documents, doctors are able to see entire patient histories, drug prescriptions, surgeries, visits, solutions, and complaints.

Look at your job and ask yourself exactly what is so unique about it that only a human can do it.

## Case Study: Using Digital Transformation for Efficiency and Profits

Cary, North Carolina, is the seventh-largest municipality in the state, with a modest population of 162,000. However, it operates like it's a major hub in Silicon Valley. Nicole

Raimundo, the CIO, has changed the way the town thinks about itself as a commodity and compares itself to other services like Google. By embarking on a platform strategy that includes field service, IT service management, marketing and collaboration tools, the town is able to get a 360-degree view of Cary's citizens (including payment, parks, and recreation class registration). The town has created an Alexa skill for Amazon Echo which allows its citizens to start the process of opening up work orders and other tools through the Echo instead of having to use the telephone. It's also using chatbots, smart lighting, smart parking, and smart recycling.

With Smart City initiatives like these, tech company Intel has suggested that smart technologies could return 125 hours to citizens every year—which equals $5 trillion[31]—along with improving the quality of life of its citizens[32]. Cary, NC, is one of the few US cities to embrace Smart City initiatives, and it's likely at the leading edge of how our services will be provided in most North American towns in the near future.

Cary is not assuming that the needs of its residents will be the same in the future. They are setting themselves up to move into the new reality by employing artificial intelligence tools such as Alexa skills and automated orders now.

Are you thinking like Cary, NC? Are you thinking about how your clients will need information in the future? Are you future focused or are you more like Blockbuster?

31   https://www.information-age.com/smart-cities-lead-cost-savings-5-trillion-123469863/

32   https://hub.beesmart.city/strategy/how-smart-cities-save-governments-businesses-citizens-money#SOURCES

## What Can We Learn from Blockbuster?

The old adage "if it isn't broken, don't fix it" will not keep us employed in the future. We have to be looking at what is around the corner, what the public wants next, what our upcoming needs may be, what our future might entail.

> Are you getting in your own way and
> blaming it on artificial intelligence? Are
> you sabotaging your own future?

That doesn't mean you need to be a futurist. It doesn't mean you need to be an inventor. It means you need to look at what has become normal and accepted and recognize that it is not likely to stay that way.

Are you getting in your own way and blaming it on artificial intelligence? Are you sabotaging your own future?

## ??? AIQ (Ask Intelligent Questions) ???

1. What has changed in the last 18 months? In the previous chapter, we asked what has changed in the last 20 to 30 years. Take a closer look and ask yourself what has changed in the last 18 months. It likely isn't much, but it could be significant. Are you working from non-traditional locations more often? Are you working longer or shorter hours? Are you answering emails and texts after hours? What new computer programs have you been introduced to, what new

certifications or workshops do you need to take based on the recent changes?

2. In the last 18 months, even the way I do grocery shopping has changed. I can now order online, I can order through my Alexa, or through voice recognition on my mobile phone. Delivery is now something I can take for granted from most locations (and we can safely assume that delivery will be available from most viable companies in the near future) whether it is through their delivery system or through a third party such as Uber Eats, Skip the Dishes, DoorDash, or GrubHub. The explosion of food prep companies such as HelloFresh, Blue Apron, and Chef's Plate has also changed the way we shop. While grocery shopping hasn't been radically altered by artificial intelligence yet, the rapid and recent developments in what was a stagnant industry have changed the way we shop, the way we plan meals, and the way we eat. Once AI gets into this space we can expect there will be even more advancements.

   Does that mean that all grocery stores and associated jobs will disappear? No. There has been a multitude of new jobs created by the recent enhancements in how we eat. Like most things, AI will replace many of the mundane tasks, allowing workers to move into jobs within the industry that require human interaction.

3. What hasn't changed over the last 18 months? Whatever hasn't changed is likely to change at some point. Can you see opportunities for yourself?

4.   I specialize in helping managers improve efficiency and effectiveness in the workplace; evolving roles is something that I take a particular interest in. I moved into computers from an administrative role in the late 1980s. I saw that computers were changing my role; I saw an opportunity, and I jumped right in. I became a computer trainer, a help-desk operator, and it launched my career in an upward trajectory. I looked at what hadn't changed, and what was expected to change over the short term, and I looked at the opportunities it provided, and decided it was an area in which I wanted to expand my skills and my role. I've never regretted that choice. Look at what is likely to change in your job as AI infiltrates it. Is there an opportunity for you to become a subject matter expert? Is there an opportunity for your skill set to expand? Look at what has not changed recently. Ask yourself if it is likely to change, and look for opportunities.

5.   Just as Cary, NC, looked at what hadn't changed but what was likely to change, do the same with your job. Don't be Blockbuster and assume you are secure where you are currently sitting.

6.   What piece of your job can only be done by you? Keep your ego out of the equation, and ask yourself if you really have something that no one (or nothing) else can offer. In the survey I conducted (referenced earlier) in September 2018, many of the respondents' comments caused me to pause. "They will always need someone to answer the phone," or "A person will always be required

for customer service," or even "A computer can't do what I do." Are you thinking this through logically, or are you really irreplaceable?

Chapter 6

## Moving Tech From Behind the Scenes to Front-and-Center

As we learned in Chapter 2, when robotics and technology were introduced into our workplaces, they were mostly behind the scenes. The rooms filled with computer equipment were seldom seen by the customer; it was the staff that interacted with them, not the customer. Today's artificial intelligence is front-and-center. It calls customers on the phone, answers their questions online, and makes them laugh, the same way a human would. This interaction is at times so effective that often customers don't even realize they are not speaking to another human.

According to market research firm Canalys, the worldwide smart-speaker market is expected to double in 2018 to 56 million units. Early figures for the year showed it tracking

16 per cent above that estimate.[33] Many brands of AI devices are already well integrated into our workplaces. Amazon has developed the Echo smart speaker, with its voice-controlled intelligent personal assistant, Alexa. Microsoft has Cortana, and Apple has Siri. Watson is a question-answering computer system developed by IBM. All of these systems are operated by using natural conversation, the same way you would speak to your co-worker, and they are designed to make our lives easier.

While some people believe that artificial intelligence will take away jobs, it's important to note that millions of new jobs are required to create this artificial intelligence. For example, myriad teams of people are behind the creation of these new voiced personal assistants. Think of the people required just to create and record the personalities (most of which have male or female options, with various accents).

According to a report by US-based research firm Gartner, AI will create more jobs than it eliminates.[34] It is predicted that by 2020, 1.8 million jobs will be eliminated, but AI will create 2.3 million jobs. By 2025, there will be a net two million jobs created. Two million jobs that don't exist right now. Two million more opportunities than we have right now. This report tells us that we will have more jobs as a result of AI, not widespread unemployment.

The team that created Microsoft's Cortana included a poet, a novelist, and a playwright. They wanted her personality to be confident, caring, and helpful but not bossy. The teams that

---

33 https://voicebot.ai/2018/05/23/google-home-beats-amazon-echo-in-q1-2018-smart-speaker-shipments-according-to-new-study/

34 https://www.gartner.com/newsroom/id/3837763

developed Apple's Siri or Amazon's Alexa created personalities that accurately reflected their companies' brands. For example, you would expect that Siri would have a bit of sassiness to her, since Apple's brand isn't as serious and conservative as some. Ask her to tell you a joke, flirt with her, or ask her if she can rap and you'll get some fun responses. Not boring nor dry, but sassy, just like Apple's brand.

A great example of how brands display different personalities are through simple emojis. When you add an emoji to a text, it may not look exactly the way it is on your phone. Depending on what kind of device the sender is using, the emoji will look a bit different. The "eye-roll face" emoji is a great example. On an iPhone, the face conveys disdain or boredom. On a Samsung smart phone, the eye-roll emoji is more of a laughing, friendly face. The face as portrayed by Google has more of an "uh-oh!" expression. One feels friendly, one feels a bit condescending, and one feels annoyed. Even the emoji for pizza is quite different from platform to platform. Apple's "pizza" emoji is a very basic pepperoni pizza. Google's has olives and pepperoni. And Samsung has done its very best to make it look yummy, with dripping cheese. Each company has spent a lot of time and money to ensure that everything they create is on-brand. The voices, the expressions, and the responses to your questions on different AI devices are quite deliberately different. This is branding and marketing in a new way, one that creates new kinds of jobs. AI will create new opportunities we can't even imagine today.

## What's in the Future for Alexa (and us)?

Alexa is already well entrenched in the workplace. As a speaker who travels internationally, talking with workers around the world, I hear a common complaint: that office workers spend too much of their day on tedious tasks, such as calendar management, online research, meetings, travel, and more. Alexa can do all of that. Alexa is stealing those jobs, or those tasks from those jobs.

Let's look at a typical scenario that might occur in the office of today:

Pradeep is a senior vice-president with a Fortune 500 company. He works from his downtown office with executive assistant James sitting outside his door to act as gatekeeper and right-hand-man.

Pradeep calls James into his office to tell him he needs to go to Washington to visit a contact at the International Monetary Fund on Friday for a 9 a.m. meeting. He plans to return that evening. Pradeep asks James to make the arrangements.

While that appears to Pradeep to be a small task, this is what James now has to do:

- Contact the travel agency (or book directly) to schedule a return flight to Washington;
- Investigate which airport is closest to the IMF (there are several airports to choose from);
- Find the details of Pradeep's favorite hotel and ensure that he can get his preferred room type for Thursday evening, and then book the hotel;

- Arrange a limo to pick up Pradeep at work to take him to the airport on Thursday, as well as pick him up at the airport Friday evening to take him home;

- Arrange a limo service to take Pradeep to the IMF on Friday morning as well as pick him up when the meeting is over;

- Cancel and rebook all of Pradeep's Friday appointments (not a simple task; it may take James several hours to find slots in Pradeep's hectic schedule to replace all his meetings with times that are compatible with the people he is meeting with); and

- Arrange a travel portfolio for Pradeep to take with him, as well as inputting all the details into his TripIt account in case of emergency.

James had no idea this new task would be thrust on him today, so the work he had planned on getting done was not getting done that day. Between fielding constant requests for Pradeep's time, co-worker interruptions, and requests for the items he was supposed to have gotten done that day, James manages it, but not easily.

The office of the future might be very different:

While Pradeep is attending a video conference meeting, Alexa is listening to the conversation. When the call is over Alexa says, "I've booked you on United Flight 983 leaving Thursday at 5:00 p.m., arriving at Reagan National Airport at 6:15 p.m. Stacy, your driver, will pick you up at the front door of the office at 3:15 p.m. on Thursday. I have reserved room

2341 for you at the Marriott, and the keyless entry for the room has been shared onto your phone.

Your car service will pick you up at your hotel at 8:25 a.m. at the front door. When you are ready to be picked up, just tell me and I will arrange to have the car come to take you back to the airport.

Your suitcase is packed and ready at home for you. I've already sent the information to Carlton, your robotic butler.

All your appointments for Friday have been rescheduled.

Would you like to spend the weekend in Washington? I can add your wife to your guest list."

And all of this would pretty much put James out of a job, wouldn't it?

Not necessarily! Which is one of the reasons you are reading this book—to find out how you can benefit from AI rather than becoming a victim of it. While artificial intelligence is certainly capable of doing many things that are being done today by humans, it doesn't mean that those people will become redundant.

I am sure that of all the things James (and any other executive assistant) does today, travel, scheduling, and the organization of an executive are not the most important, the most valuable, or the most fun. Think about how much more value James could provide Pradeep if he wasn't stuck in the administrivia of Pradeep's schedule. James knows what is going on in the office. He is more than capable of joining in on high-level discussions that take place in the company. Perhaps while Pradeep is in Washington, James can replace him in some of the meetings that are scheduled for Friday instead of having to reschedule them all. James now has the time to get the documentation organized for his boss so that Pradeep is fully informed and ready to take action during the meetings at the IMF. He can also get himself prepared to attend Pradeep's other meetings on his behalf. James can easily become Pradeep's strategic partner, offering far more intellectual value to the organization than he currently does.

## ??? AIQ (Ask Intelligent Questions) ???

1. Look around your current workplace and ask yourself, "What are the tasks I currently do that are mundane, repetitive, and could be replaced by a machine?" If it is possible for a machine to take over some of your mundane and repetitive tasks, you can be sure that someone is working on developing that capability. Consider the tasks listed in the "office of the future" above for James and Pradeep. Your AI assistant (Alexa, Watson, Siri, or whoever) is already capable of performing many of those tasks. New capabilities are being developed daily. While I predict that one day we will have robots (robotic butlers) at home to perform tasks such as packing suitcases, we already have versions of that in our homes now. I have a robotic vacuum cleaner that cleans my floors every Wednesday at 9 a.m.

2. What other value do I provide that is unique to me? Where are emotions required, and where is logic required, as well as the ability to extrapolate from that

data? Take, for instance, the borrowing of money at a bank. Right now, my husband, Warren, and I are looking at buying a new house. We went online and input our financial data into an online calculator to get a sense of how big a mortgage the bank would give us. At the end of the application, that information was sent to my bank branch, and we requested an appointment to meet with our lending specialist.

A person arranged the appointment with us on the telephone. When we went into the bank, we met with the branch's lending specialist, who discussed the standard lending structures. But because we are self-employed and we own income properties, our profile didn't fit into the standard application, so we were sent home with a list of documents to obtain, and an appointment the following week with a specialized lending representative who works with people who are self-employed.

The whole process was frustrating. I immediately knew that we wouldn't fit the typical model and would have to see a specialist. When we mentioned that fact to the person on the phone and in our email to our first lending specialist, we were told that we had to follow the procedure, to see where we stood.

Over the years, we have had many mortgages with this bank. They know our profile, our history and our finances. They even had the documents from past purchases, but we still had to go through all their steps and provide the repeated documentation.

The bank of the future will likely be slightly less frustrating. AI will automatically go through our bank accounts (personal and business), know all the money we owe, know our assets and approximate values, and know our income.

Instead of worrying that Alexa can do your job, ask yourself what you can do that she can't.

The odds are, a computer algorithm could have approved our loan immediately. However, if we had questions or issues, we would want to meet with a human. A human who would provide higher value than AI. AI can complete a lot of the routine tasks, but when the computer logic doesn't apply, only human reasoning will do. For instance, if we had one of our income properties up for sale, that would likely be a circumstance in which AI might not be appropriate.

There are so many opportunities for artificial intelligence to steal your job if you stand back and let that happen. Are there places where you can add the kind of value only a human can provide? We already know that many jobs haven't been invented yet that will be needed. Are you keeping your eyes open for the possibilities?

Instead of worrying that Alexa can do your job, ask yourself what you can do that she can't.

# Chapter 7
## Trainers, Explainers, and Sustainers

A I will, unquestionably, bring changes to the workforce. The manufacturing and transportation sectors are likely to be hit the hardest by AI, according to the Gartner report mentioned previously. Meanwhile, the public sector, healthcare, and education are expected to benefit most from the creation of new jobs.

"Robots are not here to take away our jobs, they're here to give us a promotion—I think that's the way we should start looking at AI," Manjunath Bhat, Gartner's research director, told CNBC.

> "Robots are not here to take away our jobs, they're here to give us a promotion."
> –Gartner's Manjunath Bhat on CNBC.com

We need people to perform the critical tasks that machines cannot do. There will be many jobs that are created as a result of AI. Jobs that do not exist today. Jobs that look nothing like the jobs we currently know about—jobs that we don't yet even know that we need.

AI has already created many jobs that didn't previously exist. They belong to an entirely new category of uniquely human jobs. They aren't replacing old jobs; they require skills and training that are just now being invented.

There are three new categories of AI-driven business and technology jobs that are based on humans working alongside technology. They are: *trainers*, *explainers*, and *sustainers*.

### Trainers

Trainers teach a machine to do what it needs to do. In the case of Sophia (in Chapter Two), someone needed to teach Sophia the rules of Rock, Paper, Scissors for her to know that she had beaten Jimmy Fallon in the game. When Apple created Siri, they had to teach her to have a sense of humor and to be a bit sassy. She didn't learn that on her own, she was taught.

My Alexa had to be taught to recognize my voice vs. my husband's. She had to understand how to interact with my television, my thermostat, and my lights. When I say to her, "Call Christopher," she needs to understand who he is and what phone number to reach him at. She had to be trained on what to do when I ask her to call him. Trainers aren't the same as programmers, although they might be part of the next generation of computer programmers.

Back in 1988, when I started in the computer department, I served several functions. I was primarily help desk support. When a computer didn't do what the operator thought it should do, people called me for help. I did troubleshooting and helped people get their computers to do what they needed so they could get their work done. We will still need help desk support when AI is fully functional. Albeit, not at the basic or entry level, but certainly when a situation is complicated and requires human thinking.

Language is something that needs to be interpreted—we all use it slightly differently. For instance, a *bunny hug*, in some parts of Canada, is a hooded sweatshirt. But if you ask Alexa for a bunny hug, she will assume you're referring to a type of dance popular in the early 20th Century. Yahoo is currently training its chatbots in the subtleties of human communication. When you tell their chatbot that your computer is broken, it needs to understand what you mean by broken. Does it mean the monitor is cracked, that it has crashed, or that it won't do what you want it to do? Trainers need to work with chatbots and other forms of artificial intelligence to train them in the subtleties of language.

I was also a software manipulator. I wasn't officially a programmer, but I quickly learned how to teach my software to do things automatically. I created macros and automatic functions (like Canadian spellings for spellcheck). We will still need people to create these kinds of functions for Alexa, Siri, and Cortana, as well as all versions of AI. We will need to make some of these functions industry-specific (such as working on an assembly line or answering the phone with the company name and a specific script), as well as function-specific (for instance, train Alexa that, when she hears me in the shower in the morning, it's time to turn the temperature in the house up to 21C, boil the water in the kettle for my tea, and turn the music on in the house). Someone has to train the mass-produced virtual assistants to do what we want them to do.

Trainers are also teaching AI assistants about human traits such as empathy. The MIT Media Lab has created Koko, a chatbot designed to offer emotional support. Trainers are training Koko to be empathetic in a way that seems sincere. If you say to Koko that you are having a bad day, Koko doesn't respond with a canned response like, "I'm sorry to hear that," but instead will ask for more information and offer advice. If you tell Koko you are feeling stressed, Koko might recommend that you think of that tension as a positive emotion to be channeled into action.

Chatbots are trained on typical responses they can expect to receive and then taught the answers they should provide. Someone had to train the chatbot that when a human says, "I don't understand," it needs to rephrase the question and ask it again. Someone had to teach it what "no" means, as well as, "Can I be transferred?" so the chatbot can offer the correct response. As much as the computer learns through experience the same way we do, we almost need someone to train the computer, the same way parents teach children about consequences and appropriateness.

## Explainers

Explainers are human experts who explain computer behavior to other humans. For instance, an explainer could help us understand why a self-driving car performed in a certain way. Or why we got the results we did from a computer-based machine, especially when the result was counterintuitive or controversial. In the same way a lawyer can explain why someone acted in self-defence when initially their actions seemed inappropriate, we will need explainers to tell us why a machine did what it did. If an AI unit's actions might be considered unfair, illegal, or just plain wrong, it would be the explainer who would tell us why the machine made the decision it made. This job of explainer didn't exist five years ago. Now, explainers are becoming integral to understanding why AI makes the decisions and choices that it does.

For example, when the European Union's new General Data Protection Regulation (GDPR) was implemented in May 2018, it gave consumers the right to receive an explanation for any algorithm-based decision (such as the interest rate offered on a mortgage or credit card).

Experts estimate that companies will have to create about 75,000 new jobs to administer the requirements demanded by the GDPR.[35]

Artificial intelligence will reach conclusions that we won't always understand. Think about the importance of air accident investigators being able to gain access to the black box. Without the black box, we could only make assumptions as to why things

---

35    https://hbr.org/2018/07/collaborative-intelligence-humans-and-ai-are-joining-forces

were done in a crisis. When we are guessing, we don't know for sure why things happened.

When airline captain Chesley "Sully" Sullenberger landed a passenger plane on the Hudson River in 2009, it was difficult for investigators to figure out the exact impact of the bird strike that had occurred in the plane's engines. Did Sully have enough time to return the plane to LaGuardia? Did the thrust in the engines stop immediately, or was there some left for awhile after the birds hit the engines? Fortunately, in that investigation, not only were all the passengers alive to retell the story, so were the pilot and the crew. But imagine if that hadn't been the case. Imagine if something had happened to the cockpit crew and the automatic pilot had had to take over. In cases like that, an explainer can help us determine why the automatic pilot did what it did.

Since computers can't be interviewed to explain why they did what they did (at least not yet), we will need human explainers to interpret and describe the actions of computers to non-expert users. This will be particularly important in evidence-based industries such as law and medicine, where a practitioner needs to understand how AI has weighted certain inputs. Why did it do X and not Y? What was the thinking on the part of the computer?

## Sustainers

Sustainers ensure that AI systems are functioning properly, safely, and responsibly. They also ensure that AI systems uphold ethical standards (in part to ensure that we don't ever end up with a real-life version of HAL). For instance, we need people to make sure that industrial robots don't harm humans because they don't understand that we are fragile, unlike machinery.

## The Case for Humans

Since computers follow rules, while humans learn and evolve through our experiences, there will always be jobs that only humans can do. However, computers (and therefore artificial intelligence) are learning to do things that previously could only be done by people.

Robotics, machine vision, and sensors are being used to manage global manufacturing and supply chains.

Take the US Postal Service as an example. Ninety-nine per cent of its mail sorting has been automated. That remaining one per cent needs to be done by a human because the machine cannot confidently read certain addresses if they are sloppily rendered or the packaging obscures the writing. The US Postal Service handles about 500 million pieces of mail each day. Without a human reading those exceptional envelopes, approximately five million items would not get delivered each day.

There will be jobs that will always require a human to be in the loop. Currently, we can only automate so far. When something needs to be corrected, it is usually corrected by a human, and then that exceptionality is taught to the AI system.

According to a report by Tungsten Network, a UK-based company that describes itself as a "global supply chain enabler," the average business loses nearly 6,500 working hours, or

$171,340 a year, chasing purchase order numbers, processing paper invoices, and responding to inquiries for similar items.[36]

Imagine if we could free up that money and use that time to explore opportunities for growth with existing customers and go after new ones. The potential that AI provides for the supply chain will reduce stress and wasted time, and will ultimately positively impact the economy. When something needs to be improved through human interaction or interference, we improve it and then teach our systems the new way of doing whatever we changed. We need people to make the improvement and train the system on the new improvement.

Google, Amazon, and IBM are already doing that. American consulting firm McKinsey & Company estimates that those organizations spent between $20 billion and $30 billion on artificial intelligence in 2016, with 90 per cent of that going to research and development.[37]

### ??? AIQ (Ask Intelligent Questions) ???

1. Looking at your industry or profession right now, do you see artificial intelligence starting to appear? Are there new ways of doing things, easier ways, and are any tasks you do being offloaded to an automated system?

2. Does it look like your company is sticking its head in the sand, assuming that all will be well, just like Blockbuster did?

---

36  http://www.mhlnews.com/global-supply-chain/supply-chain-losing-hours-money-poor-financial-systems

37  http://asq.org/qualitynews/qnt/execute/displaySetup?newsID=23603

Computers are a far better use of time and money when it comes to crunching big data compared with manual methods, such as a person using a calculator. Computers spot patterns quickly.

One pattern that a computer can spot instantly compared to a manual-based system is credit card use. Prior to computer-based fraud algorithms, credit card companies would have employees watch for anomalies in your spending patterns and potentially freeze your card from spending. Remember when we used to need to alert our credit card company if we were traveling? That took time. If your credit card information was stolen without your knowledge, it could take weeks for the spending to be noticed. Now, the computer spots an unusual use instantly and can freeze the card immediately.

I find this fascinating. As a professional speaker, I travel regularly. I might be in New York City in the morning and San Diego in the afternoon. I will typically use my credit card at each stop along the way. A few years ago, I had a call from my bank because they had detected unusual activity on my credit card. Since virtually all of my credit card activity is likely atypical for the average person, I was curious about what triggered the bank's call to me. It turned out that the bank's computer flagged my card because it had been used to pay for a movie, which was outside my usual spending patterns. It was outside my patterns because it wasn't me. Someone had somehow managed to capture my credit card information and was testing it to see if the card was still valid. My card was shut down by my credit card company because they accurately knew the purchase had not been made by me.

If we had people watching all of the credit card transactions that happen every day to see what looks unusual, I'm sure that using a credit card to pay for a movie wouldn't have registered on anyone's radar. But the computer was able to detect this subtle change in my credit card use.

AI can save millions of dollars a day by being able to spot fraudulent activity and freezing the user's card without approving the transaction.

Once the computer detected the problem, it turned it over to a human to deal with it. In the future, I could easily envision this scenario including a conversation with a chatbot about the purchase to determine that it was fraudulent, leaving the human in the credit card office to deal with even more complex issues.

Computers now can learn from each other, as well. They can sync information (including new findings) across networked machines, which accelerates the pace of machine learning faster than that of human learning. I would like to think that, in the workplace, if a person learns something that makes their job easier and better, they would share it with their coworkers as a matter of course. Unfortunately, we know this isn't true.

Like many people, we watch the bulk of our television through the TV and movie-streaming service Netflix. When I'm finished watching one television series, or a movie, Netflix says, "Since you've watched X, you will probably enjoy Y" and makes recommendations that are typically very accurate for me. Netflix, using artificial intelligence, uses predictive analytics to identify the types of shows and movies I enjoy. The same is true for online shopping. Companies use software to predict, based on past purchases, what you may wish to buy in the future.

And yes, people can do that too, but it requires them to have a lot of knowledge about what I have purchased in the past, as well as their own current and future inventory. Assume I am shopping at Macy's. The service representative doesn't know me and doesn't what I've bought in the past, and it wouldn't be easy for her to find that information out either. That makes it very hard for her to make recommendations on what she can offer me.

I eat out a lot. When I go to a restaurant, I like it when my server makes suggestions about what I may want to order. They ask me questions about what I like and give me advice that goes beyond the daily special. I almost always get what they suggest. I'm willing to bet that I'm not the only one who likes it when their server makes suggestions. In my experience, only servers in high-end restaurants make recommendations or tell you what their favorite dish is. When I find myself at a chain restaurant I often am told that "everything on the menu is good" without a specific recommendation at all. The inventory in a restaurant isn't extensive. There are a limited number of items on any menu—so why don't servers make suggestions more often? Why don't they pay attention to customers' orders so they can make wine or dessert suggestions?

Even though there are things that computers do much better than humans, humans still have the upper hand. There are specific skills and innate abilities that always give us an advantage over machines. Our main advantage is that we have *sensorimotor skills*. We can process what we see, hear, or touch and act accordingly. Many times, we act on our senses' input subconsciously.

I was walking down the street, about to cross at an intersection, when I heard a car horn. Without "thinking" about it, I stopped and looked up to see a car running a red light. I didn't need to consciously ask myself "why did that car honk?"—I subconsciously reacted and stopped walking. Computers can't do that.

When taking blood samples, the nurse or technician needs to be in tune with their patients to see how they are tolerating the procedure. If someone starts to panic, he may pass out. While machines are capable of taking blood, they wouldn't have the sensorimotor skills to understand the reaction of the patient and stop or soothe him while the procedure is taking place.

Our cognitive functions allow us to perceive context, learn from experience, and make decisions based on incomplete information. Computers run on rules, and those rules don't currently include cognitive functions.

However, that may soon be changing for chatbots and virtual assistants. Aida is a *virtual human* (or *cognitive agent*) used by SEB, a major Swedish bank, to interact with customers. She can handle verbal conversations, has access to vast stores of data and can answer many frequently asked questions such as how to open an account, and she can perform simple tasks like booking meetings or delivering branch information. She can also ask callers follow-up questions to help solve their problems, and she's able to analyze a caller's tone of voice (frustrated vs. appreciative, for instance) and use that information to provide better service. Whenever Aida can't resolve an issue—which happens in about 30 per cent of cases—she turns the caller over to a human customer service representative and then monitors that interaction to learn how to resolve similar problems in the future. With Aida handling basic requests, human reps can concentrate on addressing more complex issues, especially those from unhappy callers who might require extra attention.

Customer service is likely always going to require a human, even though much of it will involve automation. While the naysayers are nervous about putting human customer service agents out of work, the human agents will be able to focus on the more complex interactions.[38] The debate shouldn't be over whether cognitive agents like Aida will displace humans, it should be more of a conversation about finding ways for humans and cognitive agents to work together.

Interactive voice response (IVR) has been in existence since the 1970s, but it became vital to customer call centers in the late 1990s. Chatbots are an evolution of that technology. However, they are unable to deal with the more complicated issues because they are unable to mimic the human thinking process. In manufacturing, for example, robots are evolving from "dumb" industrial machines into smart, context-aware "cobots" (short for co-robots, a robot that is designed to work with humans). A cobot arm might, for example, handle repetitive actions that require heavy lifting, while a human performs complementary tasks that need dexterity and human judgment, such as assembling a gear motor.

Hyundai is extending the cobot concept with computerized exoskeletons. These are wearable robotic devices which adapt

---

38  https://www.tearsheet.co/modern-banking-experience/swedish-bank-seb-is-using-a-cognitive-agent-for-customer-service

to the user and enable industrial workers to perform their jobs with superhuman endurance and strength—a bit like Ironman.

Data analytics firm GNS Healthcare uses machine-learning software to collect patients' health records to identify what health interventions and drugs would be best suited or may have been previously overlooked to improve health outcomes. This approach enabled GNS to uncover a new drug interaction hidden in unstructured patient notes. GNS's CEO, Colin Hill, says that this is not garden-variety data mining to find associations.[39] "Causal modeling and simulation is the only type of technology capable of answering the 'holy grail' questions that are necessary to better match drugs and other health interventions to individual patients and discover new pathways for interventions," he said, "like finding a needle in a haystack—which cannot be done otherwise." This software can answer the questions we need answered, such as what treatment will work and at what dose for each patient.

Inflexible processes present a challenge for many organizations and Mercedes-Benz is no exception. Their most profitable customers had been requesting individual customization to their cars. A bespoke version of their car. Unfortunately, Mercedes-Benz' assembly systems couldn't deliver. "Dumb" robots had been used in traditional car manufacturing to perform automated steps in the assembly of each car. By replacing the old robots with AI-enabled cobots and redesigning its processes around the combination of human and machine, they were able to create the flexibility they needed.

---

39   https://www.outsourcing-pharma.com/Article/2016/12/06/Celgene-invests-in-GNS-Healthcare-machine-learning-platform

Cobot arms become an extension of the worker's body, which enables them to pick up and place heavy parts with less manual labor, and the system puts the worker in control of the build of each car. The flexibility of the system also allows the cobots to handle different tasks, depending on what is required, by an easy reprogram change using just a tablet. You can order your car exactly the way you want it, and Mercedes can deliver.

While flexibility is important for some companies, for others the premium is on speed. As we saw earlier, credit card fraud is one of those areas where speed matters. Companies have seconds to determine whether they should approve a transaction. If it's fraudulent, they will most likely have to cover that loss directly, which is a cost. Denying a legitimate transaction is also potentially a loss if they anger or alienate their customer. If credit card companies were habitually denying legitimate transactions, people would be likely to find a new credit card company. If credit card companies repeatedly failed to catch fraudulent activity, instead relying on the card owner to report the fraudulent activity when they noticed it on their monthly statements, people again would likely find a new credit card company.

According to the Association of Certified Fraud Examiners, a non-profit organization for fraud-detection professionals, a typical organization loses five per cent of its revenue annually—approximately $4 trillion, total, per year—to fraud.[40]

Like most major banks, HSBC has developed an AI-based system that improves the speed and accuracy of fraud detection. The AI monitors and scores millions of transactions daily, using

40   http://www.fraud-magazine.com/article.aspx?id=4295001895

data about purchase location, customer behavior, IP address, and other information to identify subtle patterns that signal possible fraud. HSBC first implemented the system in the United States, significantly reducing the rate of undetected fraud and false positives, and then rolled it out in the UK and Asia. A different AI system, used by Danske Bank, improved its fraud-detection rate by 50 per cent and decreased false positives by 60 per cent.[41] Reducing the number of false positives frees investigators to concentrate their efforts on equivocal transactions the AI has flagged, where human judgment is needed.

The fight against financial fraud is like an arms race: Better detection leads to more devious criminals, which leads to better detection, and the cycle continues. As you can imagine, this leads to a very short shelf life for the algorithms, which require continual updating. In addition, different countries and regions use different models. For these reasons, legions of data analysts, IT professionals, and experts in financial fraud are needed at the interface between humans and machines to keep the software always a step ahead of the criminals.

---

41  http://assets.teradata.com/resourceCenter/downloads/CaseStudies/
CaseStudy_EB9821_Danske_Bank_Fights_Fraud.pdf

# Chapter 8

## AI and Customer Service

You've probably already experienced a robocall. Your phone rang and you picked up—there was a pause before anyone spoke, and then a voice launched into a sales spiel. The *person* who called you wasn't a person at all, but an *artificial intelligence chatbot*. It sounded like a human and it responded to your voice fairly quickly (although you may have noticed a longer-than-human pause between your comment or question and their response). Once you realized you weren't speaking with a human, did you feel as though you had somehow been manipulated?

Many people complain about customer service departments, for a multitude of reasons. Tech firm NewVoiceMedia estimates that, in 2016, American companies with subpar customer service lost more than $62 billion in sales that went to competitors that provided better customer service.[42] They say that number has grown by at least $10 billion since then. Do you feel as a customer that you are critical of companies with poor customer service? Do you take your business elsewhere? I certainly do.

Some companies have outsourced their customer service to offshore countries where the minimum wage is vastly lower than that in the US or Canada. The service provided by these companies is sometimes poor and the security of the company uncertain, but the labor force is cheap and plentiful. It can be hard for American companies to find people who are willing to take telephone-based customer service jobs. Customers can be rude and even abusive. Telephone customer service is a difficult and often thankless job.

According to the US Bureau of Labor Statistics, in 2017 there were just over 2.7 million customer service representatives in the US, earning a mean average salary of $35,650.[43] In a recent study by tech giant Oracle, 80 per cent of sales and marketing leaders surveyed said they are currently using or plan to use chatbots in the near future.[44]

"The line-of-business that is most likely to embrace AI first will be customer service—typically the most process-oriented and technology savvy organization within most companies," Vala Afshar wrote in a 2017 article for HuffPost. Afshar is the

---

42  https://www.newvoicemedia.com/blog/the-62-billion-customer-service-scared-away-infographic

43  https://www.bls.gov/oes/current/oes434051.htm

44  https://www.oracle.com/webfolder/s/delivery_production/docs/FY16h1/doc35/CXResearchVirtualExperiences.pdf

Chief Digital Evangelist for CRM (Customer Relationship Management) firm Salesforce.

It has been well documented that many American customer service jobs have disappeared to countries like India, Mexico, and the Philippines. That has nothing to do with AI, and everything to do with the cost of labor. India and the Philippines have not replaced American jobs with chatbots and robocalls, but instead with lower-priced human interactions.

Companies need to use a combination of artificial and human intelligence—known as collaborative intelligence. Through collaborative intelligence, humans and AI enhance each other's strengths. Some things that come naturally to humans, such as common sense and humor, are difficult for machines. Things that are easy for machines, such as analyzing large amounts of data, are difficult for humans. Take language, for example. The word "time" has many meanings. It can be a specific moment (dinner-time), an experience (the time of your life), a historical period (in Medieval times) and many more things. It can be a verb, an adjective, and an adverb. Throw in the different tenses and you can see how it would be difficult for a computer to understand specifically what "time" means.

So, while AI will radically alter how work gets done and who does what, it will be about augmenting what we do, not replacing it. Researchers H. James Wilson and Paul R. Daugherty at the *Harvard Business Review* found that the most significant performance improvements occurred when humans and machines worked together.[45]

---

45  https://hbr.org/2018/07/collaborative-intelligence-humans-and-ai-are-joining-forces

Artificial intelligence in the workplace
isn't about machines or people. It is
about both complimenting each other.

The strengths of people (understanding nuances, language, and humor) were not easy for machines. But what came easy for machines (such as analyzing enormous amounts of data) was almost impossible for humans. One of the first things we need to do is understand how people can augment machines, how machines can enhance what we do, and how to redesign business processes to support that. It isn't about replacing people—it's not either/or, it's instead/and.

Artificial intelligence in the workplace isn't about machines or people. It is about both complementing each other.

A single chatbot can provide routine customer service to many people simultaneously, whereas a human can typically help only one person at a time. I find myself frustrated when I call a support line only to be told, "We are experiencing a high volume of calls. The approximate wait time is 37 minutes." In those situations, I would prefer to have the option to choose to wait to speak to a live agent, or to speak to a chatbot. I also find it frustrating when it is clear that my customer service agent is multi-tasking and supporting many chat conversations at the same time. I have found that there are long waits between answers, and that I occasionally get answers that aren't part of my conversation—the agent has responded to the wrong customer screen.

My favourite quote from poet and civil rights activist Maya Angelou is, "I've learned that people will forget what you said, people will forget what you did, but people will never forget how you made them feel." When my customer service agent makes me feel like I'm an interruption, an annoyance, or just one of many people she is dealing with, I don't feel good about my interaction with that company. A chatbot is not going to create a processing delay on an online chat. They can have numerous simultaneous conversations, with no mix-ups or slow-downs—something that people just cannot do.

As I mentioned, if I don't like the service I receive from a company, I am quick to jump to their competition. If they don't make me feel valued and important, I perceive that as poor service. The statistics reported by NewVoiceMedia suggest that I am far from alone in that.

> "I've learned that people will forget what you said, people will forget what you did, but people will never forget how you made them feel."
> –Maya Angelou

While on a business trip, I found myself stranded at Dulles International Airport in Washington. My plane had been canceled, after repeated delays, and I knew that it was going to be difficult to get a flight out within the next few days.

I called my airline, only to be put into a very long queue. The estimated wait time was 65 minutes. All I needed was to have my name automatically listed for the next available flight to my destination. (For some reason, the computer terminals at the airport were unable to do that.) A chatbot would have been perfect in that situation. Imagine the airlines using chatbots to calculate the best route and the passengers' preferred flight times, and book them automatically on another flight. All 300 of my fellow passengers could have been rebooked in a matter of minutes, instead of the hours that it took for all of us to do it separately, by human operators. If I had wanted to reroute to a different destination or felt that I had a grievance with the airline, I could have waited online (or in line at Dulles) to speak a person. I didn't need a person for my rebooking; I just needed to know what time my new flight was.

The future of great customer service is artificial intelligence. In a 2018 article in *Forbes* magazine, Blake Morgan, a self-described Customer Service Futurist, estimates that by 2025, 95 per cent of customer interactions will be supported by AI technology.[46] According to research firm Gartner, businesses around the world will increase in value by $1.2 trillion in 2018 because of their use of AI. This, they say, is 70 per cent higher than the increase that occurred in 2017.

As those numbers tell us—and they are likely to climb even higher next year—AI technology is affecting the way customers interact with brands. Already, many companies are using chatbots to allow customers to place orders for goods and services.

I have a chatbot set up on my Facebook page to help customers connect to me, place orders for training or my books, or to receive bonus materials after visiting my business page. To test it, go to my ON THE RIGHT TRACK Facebook page (https://www.facebook.com/RhondaScharfONTHERIGHTTRACK)

---

46  https://www.forbes.com/sites/blakemorgan/2018/02/08/10-customer-experience-implementations-of-artificial-intelligence/#30a26a8d2721

and click on the blue SEND MESSAGE button. Then simply follow the prompts. Now, it's quite clever but it's not AI. It uses preprogrammed (by me) responses to inquiries that I get on my Facebook page. It has a script and it doesn't move outside of the script. Yet. How long will it be until my extremely basic chatbot can comprehend what you are asking and respond as a live human would? While my chatbot is not an example of artificial intelligence, there are some that are. Ticketmaster has implemented AI to combat ticket fraud, although they acknowledge that it is a constant battle. They were able to create a bot to fight *scalper bots* that buy blocks of tickets and resell them at a higher price. Ticketmaster invests millions of dollars a year to combat scalper bots.[47]

Domino's Pizza has a Facebook Messenger chatbot named Dom that allows customers to place an order simply by sending a message that says "pizza." Dom can gather all the details for your pizza faster than if you had placed a call to the restaurant. Prior to the launch of Dom, Domino's had simplified ordering pizza by launching an "Easy Order" feature. Through the use of an Apple Watch or on the Domino's website, all the hungry buyer needs to do is press a button and their pizza is ordered. Since Dominos started using a chatbot to take food orders in 2016, virtually all of its major competitors, as well as many smaller, local pizza chains, have followed suit.

These chatbots are very similar to my ON THE RIGHT TRACK chatbot on my Facebook page. They allow the company

---

47    https://www.theglobeandmail.com/arts/music/after-years-of-criticism-ticketmaster-hopes-to-be-hero-in-fight-against-scalpers/article35272624/

to make ordering pizza as simple as possible. Ultimately, the consumer wants things to be easier. They don't want to wait on hold, have a frustrating conversation with someone who doesn't understand their problem, and then have to go through it all over again before they have their issue resolved or are able to find the product or service they want to buy.

*Click, click, send.* How easy is that, and how much more satisfied does it make the consumer?

Spotify, Netflix, and Amazon are particularly good at looking at their customers' past history to make recommendations based on what they've watched, listened to, or purchased. Google Photos will automatically label my photos based on the people in them (it recognizes faces), and the location or date they were taken, as well as landmarks, the type of photo (such as a birthday celebration, wedding, an animal, or food). Google Photos can even automatically generate albums or animate photos into quick videos. Imagine creating a video for your parents' 50th anniversary party based on the photos you took—it's a reality, now.

KFC in Beijing has taken automated service a step further by implementing technology that uses facial recognition software to recognize their customers. KFC has teamed up with Baidu, a search engine often referred to as "China's Google," to develop technology that can be used to predict people's orders. Their automated service will estimate how old you are (which apparently helps them decide if you would want chicken, salad, fries, or coleslaw, based on their algorithms), and will actually perceive your mood (perhaps a smile indicates you want a salad and a grimace indicates you want French fries). Based on that input, the system will make suggestions for your meal. The kiosk can also recognize that the customer has used the system before, remember what they've ordered in the past, and make recommendations based on their ordering history. This facial recognition technology is planned to be expanded to KFC's 5,000 stores across China.

Imagine walking up to a kiosk to order your lunch. As you stand in front of the machine, it says "Hi Rhonda. Welcome back. Do you want to order the same two-piece chicken leg lunch with fries and a diet Coke that you asked for yesterday, or are you more interested in a side salad with your chicken today?"

Some people might find that a wonderful time-saver, and some might be offended that the system offered them a salad instead of fries. But it knows you, it knows your ordering patterns, and it feels like it's saving you time and effort, doesn't it?

LivePerson is a New York-based company that provides AI-augmented messaging. They earned roughly $200 million in 2017, working with IBM's Watson supercomputer. They claim that approximately 50 per cent of all customer service interactions are highly suitable for bots. Eight out of 10 customers they surveyed said they prefer messaging (online text chat) to phone-based customer service (voice) and that customer satisfaction rates dramatically increase when a company uses messaging rather than the telephone.[48] They see very simple questions being handled by a bot, but once the conversation

---

48   https://info.liveperson.com/AI-powered-Conversational-Web-on-demand.html?aliId=64071503

becomes complicated, it is escalated to a human agent to deal with. Once the challenging aspect of the situation is handled by the human agent, the call can be transferred back to the bot to complete any simple details.

I can attest that my own adult children would prefer that as well. If I need to reach them, I can text them or send them a Snapchat, but calling them will quickly find me leaving a voice mail for them. I know that when I'm surfing the net, I'm much happier to use an online chat to get the answers to my questions, over picking up the phone and waiting for help-desk support.

Does messaging feel faster and more efficient to you? You can stay focused on the issue at hand, get responses quickly, and feel that you've been heard. A telephone often leaves us stuck on hold, taking longer to get the information, and sometimes feeling as though we need to make a bit of small-talk with the person on the other end before we get to our issue. With online chat, we can be more blunt and direct, getting right to our question.

## Using AI to Address Customers' Pain Points

> The biggest differentiator of success
> is the customer experience.

Customer service has radically changed in the digital age. We know that customers aren't as loyal as they used to be to brand, product, or even price. The biggest differentiator of success is the customer experience.

Take a look at your business and identify where your customers' pain points are. Where is the customer experience failing your customers? Do a mystery shop and pretend you know nothing about your business and try to find what you need by exploring, with no inside knowledge of the company or its product lines. Look at your website with fresh eyes. Look at your storefront, your telephone system, your ordering system. Where do your customers stumble? What is the most inconvenient aspect of doing business with you, from their perspective? Don't listen to your own excuses, and don't explain or justify. Look at the entire process through the eyes of a brand-new customer. Identify where the pain points are for customers and ask yourself if there is a way you can make the pain points go away.

Amazon Go has done an excellent job of optimizing the process of grocery shopping (both online and in person). They evaluated what consumers liked and didn't like about buying groceries, and their research showed that the pain point for grocery shopping is the checkout experience. People dislike waiting in lines and dislike the entire process of paying for their groceries. So they installed ceiling-mounted sensors and cameras backed by artificial intelligence. It enables them to track what you pick up and put in your bag, or put back on the shelf. When you are finished walking around the store, you simply *leave*. Just like with the 1-Click Ordering system they offer for online shopping, you are charged for what you walk out of the store with; purchases are automatically charged to the credit card you have linked to the Amazon Go app. They have minimized the pain point of the shopping checkout.

Netflix looked at their main pain point, which was bandwidth issues in emerging markets. Using AI algorithms, they review each frame of a video so they can compress it. But they compress it only to the degree necessary, without affecting image quality. This method, called Dynamic Optimization not only improves streaming quality over slower speeds, it also tailors content for viewing on tablets and mobile phones.

Online gourmet food gift retailer 1-800 Flowers was one of the first retailers to embrace AI to improve the customer experience, while at the same time increasing revenue by using conversational chatbots. The pain point they were alleviating was a frustrating and confusing ordering system. Although the name of the company implies they sell only flowers, they offer much more, including gourmet foods and gifts. Their online ordering process became too cumbersome and they needed an easier system. Now, they use IBM's Watson supercomputer to offer GWYN (Gifts When You Need), which has transformed their online experience for customers. According to IBM, GWYN is a "conversational commerce engine"—a smart virtual shopping assistant that intuitively guides customers through their shopping experience, to select the right gift.[49] GWYN asks questions to make the right recommendations. She asks what the occasion is, what the sentiment is, and what types of things the recipient likes (roses, lilies, chocolates). The more interaction between GWYN and the customer, the smarter GWYN becomes. Online tech magazine *Digiday* reported that

---

49  For more information about GWYN, read IBM's Retail Industry Blog article, GWYN Gives the Gift of Simplicity: https://www.ibm.com/blogs/insights-on-business/retail/gwyn-gives-gift-simplicity/.

just two months after Gwyn's Facebook launch, 70 per cent of the company's chatbot orders came from brand new customers, who were younger than their typical customers.[50]

Then, 1-800 Flowers took AI a step further and teamed up with Amazon Alexa. All you have to do is say, "Alexa, ask 1-800 Flowers to send a box of chocolates to my wife on Valentine's Day," and it will be done. By integrating AI into their customer experience, 1-800 Flowers has attracted tens of thousands of new customers. And as Facebook CEO Mark Zuckerberg says, "It's pretty ironic: To order from 1-800-Flowers, you never have to call 1-800-Flowers again."

## ??? AIQ (Ask Intelligent Questions) ???

It is clear that the technology that currently exists can make the customer experience better. Are you thinking about your customers and making their lives easier and better, or are you just offering excuses about why things need to stay the same? Your use of AI needs to serve a purpose relative to your customer's purchasing experience.

1. Are there existing products and services (like chatbots) that could make your customer's life easier? What is your ability to automate? I don't mean to imply that you have the ability yourself to create a chatbot, but where are the areas that automation would make the customer experience better? Is a kiosk possible, a

---

50  https://digiday.com/marketing/two-months-1-800-flowers-facebook-bot-working/

chatbot, an automated service? Does it need to be done the way you are doing it? Has someone else invented something that would benefit you and your company?

2. Are there places to shift your staff higher up on the value chain? According to a 2016 McKinsey report, less than 30 per cent of a customer representative's role can be automated at this point.[51] You will still need your customer service representatives, but is there a way to use their abilities and skills higher on the value chain in your organization? Remove the time-consuming tasks that a bot can easily handle, and maximize your human impact. Instead of having your customer service representatives directly on the front lines, ask yourself if a chatbot could handle even some of the basic inquiries, concerns, and orders, leaving your customer service team to handle the more complex situations? This will not only make your service response time faster (which makes customers happy), but the human-to-human contact will be implemented in those situations that need the personal touch.

3. If your business is online, identify (via your analytics) where the highest percentage of your customers are leaving your website. If your business is direct contact, at what point do you see customers leaving your store without purchasing anything? Do you notice that when the checkout line exceeds three customers, other customers turn and leave the store without a purchase? If your phone queue is more than four minutes long,

---

51 Link to 2016 McKinsey report.

do you find that your hang-up rates are higher? Only by identifying where you are losing customers can you make the adjustments necessary to address your pain points and improve your customer experience.

It is painful, but really examine your analytics to determine where you aren't quite as good as you could be. Every person and every organization has the ability to improve. If you need help in understanding those analytics, get help. But figure out where your customers aren't loving the process. Find out where you can make it better.

4. Identify which questions your customers are repeatedly asking, and how you can address those concerns or questions. Continually answering the same question is an obvious cue that you have a pain point. (And no, posting that information in the FAQ section of your website will not be enough to alleviate that pain point.)

5. What pain points can you address by implementing artificial intelligence?

6. Would a mobile app, an improved call center, or chatbots improve your customer's experience? Do you have a team member who monitors your social media for complaints as well as kudos? Do you reach out to connect with them and address people's concerns?

While using AI for your customer experience can certainly make for better customer service, you may have a legitimate fear that it will create the need for layoffs. It has been suggested by Forbes.com that as many as 2.3 million American cashiers could be impacted by AI with systems such as Amazon Go and online grocery shopping and meal services.[52] But let's flip that around and look at the positive side of making your customer's experience better. Think of the demand for engineers and computer scientists who will design the systems. Think of the technicians who will install and repair them. Think about the jobs required to handle the troubleshooting.

There are elements of grocery shopping that Amazon Go currently can't handle, such as buying fresh produce and meat. They haven't figured out how to do that yet, which implies there is room for development and growth as well. Add into the mix the growth of online meal services such as Hello Fresh! and Blue Apron. They are creating new jobs in areas such as developing recipes and menus, sourcing local and organic produce that many of these options provide. Chatbots and technology can handle much of the taking care of online issues, freeing up human employees to deal with higher value functions.

Alexa isn't stealing your customer service jobs. Artificial intelligence is making customer service even better than before.

---

52  https://www.forbes.com/sites/justcapital/2018/02/01/amazon-go-and-the-2-3-million-cashiers-it-could-leave-behind/#257204347bcc

Chapter 9

## AI and HR—a Match Made in Heaven

I met my husband, Warren, through an online dating app. When I set up my profile, I indicated the types of things that I was looking in a potential partner, such as height, a non-smoker, within a certain geographical area, and language. The algorithm the online dating site used paired me with potential matches based on the individual criteria of its members. I appeared on Warren's search, yet he did not appear on mine. He reached out to me through the site, and eventually we ended up meeting, dating, falling in love, and getting married. My parents were horrified that I would find a potential mate that way. My friends found it amusing, and I was grateful that dating companies existed, because meeting compatible men wasn't easy for me since I was self-employed and always traveling.

There are a lot of parallels between today's hiring practices and finding a mate. In the past, when you needed an employee, you might be lucky enough to have someone recommended to you (like a blind date set up by a friend). But if you didn't, you had to reach out blindly and hope the right person read your ad and applied for your job.

After that, the process involved placing an ad in the newspaper, and then using online hiring sites. And, because it relied on self-selection (like the early dating sites did), you would get interest from a lot of the wrong people. It was a time-consuming process, because someone needed to sort through all the job applications and interview multiple people; the cost to hire was exorbitant.

I went on a few dates that were a complete waste of my time before I met Warren. Imagine if, instead of me going on many dates looking for Mr. Right, I only needed to go on a handful, because nearly every candidate was an excellent match. I could be assured that no matter who I picked, things would work out.

While that certainly takes the romance out of dating, the fact that the success ratio is exponentially higher than traditional dating is compelling. Applied to the hiring process, that system is even more compelling—not to mention time and energy efficient in the short term (while hiring), but more importantly, in the long term, with improved retention rates.

According to Shervin Khodabandeh, partner and managing director with Boston Consulting Group, AI-powered relationship bots could one day be used to predict qualities such as trustworthiness and other traits that would normally require direct, personal experience to determine. Having this information up front could help predict the success of a future relationship.

Think of how this would apply to dating sites in the future. You input your criteria, exactly as I did when I met Warren, answer prepared survey questions or participate in an interview, and then wait for your Prince Charming or Princess Charming, who would automatically appear for you. The system would do an instant search and present you with several excellent and compatible candidates to choose from. Each candidate would have a score beside their profile which would predict how successfully the two of you would match. It sounds a bit like an arranged marriage and perhaps not too romantic, but knowing that the two of you are guaranteed to be compatible takes away a lot of the fear and uncertainly of dating.

Similarly, Human Resources could apply the same technology and the same process. Artificial Intelligence has already proven itself to be invaluable in many HR functions. Whether it is scanning resumes for key phrases or skills, providing feedback to candidates, scheduling interviews, or identifying the top candidate, AI can save a lot of time-consuming labor—and expense—for HR.

Currently, AI is well established on the recruitment side of hiring. Chatbots are used to answer candidates' questions, schedule follow-up calls and meetings, and not only begin to establish relationships but also create a feeling of goodwill about the company. There are even companies—like Seattle-based Textio—that use AI to figure out exactly what words to put in job advertisements in order to attract the perfect candidates. Crafting the perfect job ad is especially important in a world where the competition for the best talent is fierce. Textio has analyzed millions of job postings and evaluated the candidates who applied for those jobs. It uses a predictive engine (much like a spell-check or a grammar checker on your word processing application), to analyze your job post and indicate, based on how other job descriptions have performed, whether your posting is using sentences that are too short or too long, contains confusing corporate clichés, or contains too many questions. Then, you can edit the post accordingly and be confident it will have maximum appeal to the right candidates.

Once the ad has been written, HR can rely on AI to ensure that the ad appears to their target candidates via the appropriate social media. Candidates don't have to be actively looking for a job or visiting traditional job posting sites, but instead can be watching YouTube and have "the perfect job" appear in their feed.

In the same way that, while I may not be consciously looking to buy a new car, an ad might grab my attention and cause me to think about buying a new car, a job ad may catch someone's eye even if they weren't actively looking to change jobs. If an interesting job flashes across the right person's screen, they may decide to look into it. Once they look into it, they might become interested, or they may know someone else who might be interested.

A company's fabulous, AI-augmented advertisement can catch the interest of the right potential candidates because that's what it was designed to do. Perfectly targeted ads, using the specific wording that grabs the attention of the right candidate, is the goal and, with AI, it is much more likely. If the right candidate decides to look into the job opportunity and follow through on the application process, then the first step of AI job recruiting has been successful.

Video job interviews are quickly becoming the norm in the hiring process. Once a candidate has responded to the job advertisement and has been vetted by HR, the next step is often a live video interview (on a platform such as Skype or Zoom). The hiring company will either ask live, interview-style, pre-hire assessment questions, or request that the candidate submit an introduction video. That video will be scanned by an AI-driven platform such HireVue to determine things such as eye movement (which may indicate that the candidate is regularly looking away from the screen to cue cards or another person), or even other voices in the video, which would indicate the candidate is being prompted by someone about what to say. A human might not pick up on those subtle things and recognize that the candidate perhaps doesn't know everything she says she knows. HireVue examines body language, tone of voice, and key words and compares the video interview to its existing best employees in a particular role. It then provides each candidate with a score showing what percentage of the qualities of the perfect candidate the video represented.

Korn Ferry, an international strategic consulting firm, recently surveyed nearly 800 HR professionals in reference to artificial intelligence in the recruitment process. Sixty-three per cent of those surveyed said that artificial intelligence has already changed the way they recruit. According to the survey, AI streamlines the recruiting process through candidate sourcing and applicant screening as well as the scheduling of interviews. Each of these tasks is time-consuming. AI frees up HR professionals and recruiters for other, higher-value, tasks. When identifying the best candidate for a posted job, bots such as Arya (AI recruiting software developed by Raleigh, NC-based Leoforce) scan through thousands of resumes to identify the best candidates. Arya is able to adapt and learn which candidates are best suited to the position, by analyzing company data such as performance reviews, turnover rates, and promotion data (timing and frequency).

*Fortune* magazine published an article about software that can analyze intangible human qualities and assess how well a candidate will fit in with a company's corporate culture.[53] In addition, the software strips out any distinguishing racial or gender features of the candidates, ensuring that candidate recommendations are not affected by the unconscious preferences or biases that all humans exhibit.

AI screening, along with facial recognition and voice recognition, together with a ranking algorithm, can determine which candidate most resembles the ideal candidate for a particular role.

Chatbots, which, as we have seen, have become instrumental to customer service departments, now can assist HR as well, with recruitment and information sharing. They can answer questions regarding payroll, vacation allotment, benefits, and other information-based HR questions, leaving the company's HR professionals to handle more of the human aspects of HR and fewer of the routine question-and-answer tasks that would otherwise consume large blocks of HR's time.

---

53

Chatbots are available 24/7, so when an employee is sitting at home on a Saturday night planning her family vacation, she can engage with an online chatbot and find out exactly how much vacation allotment she has for the next year instead of waiting to call HR on Monday morning to find out.

Onboarding is another time-consuming task for HR professionals that can be easily handled by AI. It can allocate office space, provide the new employee with a laptop and cell phone, a passcode, and it can even order business cards if needed, allowing the company's HR professionals to focus on more strategic tasks that have a bigger impact on the overall success of the onboarding process.

> Submitting a resume by mail or relying on traditional job-hunting methods may not help you find your next job. Where does AI go looking for the perfect employee? Websites, LinkedIn (with multiple profiles), and online resume sites as well as information gathered from social media sites such as Twitter and Facebook.

Another way HR uses AI is to identify employees who are not performing up to company standards. It can track an employee's computer activity (emails, keystrokes, Internet surfing) and measure it against a baseline of normal activity patterns within the organization to identify anomalies.

Alexa might not be stealing your job and automating it, but she may identify that you are not performing up to expectations, and tattle on you. Think about what this information could do. Your company could quickly spot areas in need of improvement using AI which automatically recognizes (and reports to the boss) that you habitually submit requests late, or that other employees often need to follow up on your work.

Consider Michelle, the fictional VP of Sales at NewCo, Inc. Traditionally, sales managers are measured on the dollars they bring into an organization. If there was automated software on Michelle's laptop and mobile phone, HR would know that she emails her executive assistant 36 times a day to ask for things that have already been loaded into her travel itinerary (thereby wasting her EA's time). That she doesn't update the company's Customer Relationship Management software often enough (she takes one afternoon a month and updates all her client files instead of doing updates after each meeting). That she routinely double-books herself for client meetings and needs to cancel things at the last minute. And that she hasn't exchanged any emails with her sales team in weeks. While the sales team may be performing well, the data will show that they are performing well *in spite of* Michelle, whose movements, tracked by AI, show that she is inefficient, not detail-oriented enough, and quite possibly not the right person to be in charge of Sales. Perhaps the sales team would do better under a different VP.

In Customer Service, AI could analyze when an issue arises, such as an error in the billing system, a fault with a product, or a location with repeated complaints. It wouldn't be up to the customer service representative to report that there have been a lot of calls complaining about the New Jersey site; the system would know that there were too many complaints, based on the notes input into the system, and it would then go on to either alert someone to that fact, or fix it.

### ??? AIQ (Ask Intelligent Questions) ???

1. Look at your internal systems and identify the pain points. Do you have your team members spending an inordinate amount of time doing things that could be automated? Have you done basic diagnostics such as time logs to identify where time is lost each day? Have you asked your team where they think we can be more efficient?

2. Are there systems in place—such as chatbots—that can be used for internal efficiencies? Can you think of any external systems that are already in place that can be used for internal use? With a little manipulation you might be able to use an existing system for a dual purpose.

3. Perhaps a new role in your company (or for you) would be to do the business analysis to identify exactly where a company is doing things manually when it could be automating them. Or be the person who investigates what is available for your company. Then, get on the implementation team. If you don't have someone at your company who can do this, you will likely need to find an outside consultant who can help you. This is an example of a job that is created from artificial intelligence. Be the expert in your office who can

identify where there is room to improve and what solutions already exist that you can implement.

Chapter 10
## AI and Efficiency

## Marketing and Advertising Efficiency

A rtificial intelligence is being used extensively in the marketing and advertising world. Netflix uses an AI-based recommendation engine (or system) that takes into consideration not just what you've watched, but also how many times you've watched something and whether you've used rewind and fast-forward during the program.

> "A recommender system [is an] information filtering system that seeks to predict the *rating* or *preference* a user would give to an item."
> –Wikipedia

143

AI is also used for programmatic advertising (the ads you see on Facebook are different from the ads I see), market forecasting, and speech recognition (also known as conversational commerce, such as speaking to Alexa and asking her to order you an Uber).

News organizations BuzzFeed and *The New York Times* have reportedly found success using algorithms to track and predict how content performs online. *The Economist* magazine and *The Wall Street Journal* use AI to manage their editorial workplaces and supply up-to-date news data. Correspondents for the news service Reuters used AI to crowd-source and fact-check up-to-the-minute information during the Mandalay Bay shooting in Las Vegas in 2017, giving them an "eight- to 60-minute head start" on the competition, according to Reg Chua, Reuters' Executive Editor for Editorial Operations, Data and Innovation.[54]

## Robot Reporters

Would you be surprised to discover that some the articles you read in *Forbes* magazine, by the Associated Press or in your Yahoo fantasy football report were written by a robot? In 2016, content generation company Automated Insights wrote 1.5 billion stories for news outlets.[55] This US-based technology firm creates articles, using sports and finance data and information, that look and sound like they were written by a human.

---

54   https://agency.reuters.com/en/insights/articles/articles-archive/reuters-news-tracer-filtering-through-the-noise-of-social-media.html

55   https://en.wikipedia.org/wiki/Automated_Insights

If AI can create job descriptions that capture the attention of the right candidates, it stands to reason that the same algorithms can produce marketing and editorial content that efficiently targets a specific demographic.

The personalization of content is something that companies like Adobe have been delivering. Not personalization like the "Hi, <insert name here>" emails we are all accustomed to receiving, but personalization of message to specific, very targeted, audiences. Twelve years ago, SAS Airlines started using Adobe Campaign, which is an Adobe Marketing Cloud solution. It allowed SAS's regional marketing departments to personalize and localize the messages they send to specific customer profiles.

Remember my earlier example about searching online for Sydney hotels? The next morning, I received an email in my inbox letting me know that hotels were on sale and flights were selling. That's a good example of the kind of thing SAS does. If they notice that someone searched flights but didn't book, they can follow up with them and reach out with a message or a deal. If a client is booked on a flight to Florida and a hurricane is approaching, they let their travelers know. Since SAS has implemented this personalized content, they say their marketing programs have become more efficient and effective. They say they have more loyal frequent flyers, higher revenue per passenger and increased customer lifetime value.[56]

## Office Efficiency

Slack is cloud-based project management software that allows teams to collaborate and share information. Niles is a Slack

---

56   https://www.adobe.com/customershowcase/story/sas.html

add-on that listens to and records conversations that take place on the Slack platform. Every time someone sends a message, Niles learns. Users can ask Niles questions, and because the information it learns is stored in a database, Niles can respond with an appropriate answer. If for some reason Niles doesn't know an answer, as soon as it is provided Niles retains it for future use. Like humans, Niles learns by experience.

American workers spend, on average, only 40 per cent of their time on their primary duties, according to a survey by technology firm Workfront, entitled *The State of Work Report 2018*.[57] The rest is spent on simple tasks like email management, booking conference rooms, and arranging meetings.

These are the kinds of tasks that can most easily be done by AI. Already, there are AI software tools like Indeavor's Workloud which can automatically add appointments to an electronic calendar. Alexa for Business can book a conference room following a simple audio command. Evie.ai is software that uses natural language processing technology to let you to book appointments, schedule a meeting room and track to-dos. It can handle multiple time zones and even CRMs such as Salesforce all through a single email or chat that you send to it.

The technology exists. Are you using it?

Many executive assistants spend an inordinate amount of time each day organizing their executive's email. While that task may be important, many EAs cite this as one of the most frustrating, unrewarding, and time-consuming tasks in their day. Again, it is the type of task AI does well.

57   https://www.workfront.com/blog/state-of-work-2018

For many companies, handling email from customers is a job done by people in customer service, who read every email they get in order to determine what their customer wants and how to deal with it. Software firm DigitalGenius, Inc. offers "an AI platform that puts your customer support on autopilot by understanding conversations, automating repetitive processes and delighting your customers," according to its website. Its technology scans and tags email and directs it to the right place within the company, where it can be dealt with.

When I am delivering a workshop on efficiency or time management, I make sure I spend time on how to handle email more efficiently—whether it's employees' own email or executives' email. Even using cut-and-paste, insert a block (a feature in Word that automates certain repeated words or phrases), and other clever hacks which, in my experience, most executives don't do, email still eats up a substantial amount of time in the day. If you're doing things like handling email yourself rather than automating the task, you are taking too much time, likely experiencing too much frustration, and not maximizing your ability to provide the most value to your company.

Magoosh, an online college test prep company, is a prime example of how DigitalGenius's AI software can enhance customer service. According to Magoosh, their AI system from DigitalGenius makes their customer service team significantly more efficient in classifying, tagging and re-routing requests. As a result, the number of customer requests waiting for a reply has been cut in half. Magoosh has been able to meet their internal service goal of responding to all customers within 24 hours. According to DigitalGenius, 83 per cent of incoming requests at Magoosh are supported by their system. These types of AI-enabled applications are in their infancy. In a few years, this market will explode, exponentially, alleviating the time-consuming administrative duties that most workers spend too much time on every day.

Are you maximizing your future by learning how these systems work early on or are you waiting until you are forced to use these time-saving technologies? Do you reject or embrace artificial intelligence?

The World Economic Forum's *The Global Shapers Survey 2017* found that nearly 80 per cent of the millennials who participated in the survey believe that artificial intelligence and technology are creating jobs rather than destroying jobs.[58]

Fifty per cent of the global population is under the age of 30. However, 50 per cent of the workforce is not under 30 and the attitudes of those in the workplace are quite different from those of our future generations.

My father is a 75-year-old retired electrician. I offered to get him an Amazon Echo or Google Home. Never having worked in an office, he was unfamiliar with the term *virtual assistant* or even *AI assistant*, and his knee-jerk reaction to the idea of having one is that he didn't want one. And I know why. He has no idea what they could do for him. He is afraid of the unknown, and he's unwilling to learn about a new "gadget."

However, my mother is still employed, works with computers, is comfortable on her own computer, and is fairly

58  http://shaperssurvey2017.org/static/data/WEF_GSC_Annual_Survey_2017.pdf

knowledgeable about technology. I offered to buy her an Amazon Echo so she could use Alexa for entertainment, to keep track of her shopping list (and even order groceries for her), and otherwise provide a little support in making her life easier. She, too, turned down my offer. Her reason? "Why would I have a computer do something that I can do myself?"

Now, I know that my parents are not statistically representative of the senior population as a whole, but this casual, anecdotal survey confirms my gut feeling—and, likely yours—that there is a segment of the population that simply resists the advancement of technology, including AI. Is it because they are afraid, or perhaps because they just cannot justify adding something else into their life? Are there other reasons they are resisting artificial intelligence in their life? The old adage "If it isn't broken, don't fix it" is true for many people; if they haven't needed a virtual assistant at this point, why do they need one now?

## Emotional Manipulation–The Storytelling Project

Humans are certainly capable of emotional manipulation. Now, it appears as if machines have learned to manipulate us, as well.

The Center for Future Storytelling at the MIT Media Lab in Boston used technology to make stories (including movies, corporate promos, or even advertising) more interactive, improvisational, and social. Some people believe they revolutionized the way stories are told. They trained machines to manipulate human emotions by "teaching" AI how to develop a narrative arc. By gathering positive and negative comments and audience reactions to thousands of sample video clips and short movies, they say their networks predicted what the audience response to a film will be, on a second-by-second basis.

As part of the Media Lab training, The Storytelling project was created. The group studied the opening sequence of *Up*, a 3D computer-animated film produced in 2009 by Pixar Animation Studios and released by Walt Disney Pictures. The movie focuses on a grumpy old man named Carl. After his wife dies, Carl attaches thousands of balloons to his house to float it to South America. Since the backstory is complicated, the opening sequence provides a silent (only the movie's music score plays) yet quick, way to provide context as to why Carl is flying to South America. The algorithm was able to map out the arc of scenes and rate them based on their negative or positive emotional impact with the audience. Volunteers were asked to annotate move clips with various emotional labels, and identify which video elements (dialogue, music, or images) triggered their responses. With these insights, AI models were refined and a simple formula was created.[59]

What does that mean to you and me? The next Hollywood blockbusters we see in the movie theater might manipulate our emotions to make us feel exactly the way they want us to feel, to ensure the success of the movie.

Is that just good filmmaking, or is it emotional manipulation? Before you answer—didn't Disney effectively do the same thing with its animations? They had a formula they repeated over and over again, very successfully. You could spot the princess, spot the sidekick, there was a soundtrack, and always ultimate tear-

[59] An excellent *Variety* article, 2017, about "Up" and AI. https://variety.com/2017/digital/news/ai-emotional-arcs-mit-mckinsey-1202635570/

jerker scenes. They had amusing scenes to break up the tension. And, of course, the famous Disney "happy ending." Were we manipulated, or did we just understand that Disney has a formula that works—and even knowing that, we can simply enjoy the film anyway? Of course, it does become a bit more complicated because Disney films are typically aimed at young children, who may not recognize the Disney formula when they see it.

Looking at literature, aren't fiction authors guilty of the same thing? Danielle Steele, James Patterson, and Stephen King each have a winning formula that is predictable and successful. So, should we be angry that AI is being used to create films that will elicit the precise reaction the producers are hoping for, or should we be happy to know that when we spend our money at the ticket booth for a movie, we are going to get exactly what we want?

Artificial intelligence will allow us, theoretically anyway, to design the perfect office. The smart phone in your pocket (or your Fitbit or Apple Watch) will know which path you take to go to the work restroom, how often you go, how long you are there, and what you do on the way there and the way back. It will know that you spend eight minutes a day chatting with Liz in Accounting, and that your vital signs elevate when you are near Greg, indicating that you dislike (or really like) Greg. It will know if you like music in your workspace, what temperature you prefer, and whether you get frustrated when coworkers are chatting near you.

Theoretically, AI could design an office that fits you perfectly. It would be the perfect temperature, have access to the perfect amount of sunlight and co-worker proximity, and put your desk as far away from (or as close to) Greg as possible.

This doesn't sound painful, doesn't it? But perhaps your feelings about Greg are actually good for your creativity so your proximity shouldn't be changed. Or perhaps when your office is just slightly too cold, you are more productive. And maybe having to walk just a bit too far to the restroom is better for your health. Is contriving the perfect environment really ideal? Isn't working with people who challenge us (or staying away from people who complement us a little too much) good for our personal and professional growth? Do we really want a "perfect" office environment?

## ??? AIQ (Ask Intelligent Questions) ???

1. What is a small and repetitive task that you are currently doing, that would be better suited for a computer to do? For instance, booking flights, writing to-do lists, filing. Once you've automated the smaller repetitive tasks, you can focus on other tasks that require more effort with a higher return to your organization.

2. Is there a way that you can utilize a system such as Alexa for Business in your workplace? Examples where this could be helpful include scheduling upcoming meetings, adjusting the temperature in the meeting room, booking a conference room, or ordering in lunch for the meeting. If you've ever spent any time at all doing these things you've probably rolled your eyes and

been frustrated how long these seemingly unimportant tasks take. Time that, surely, could be better spent.

## Chapter 11
## Your Future is up to You

Adapting to the new mindset about AI will be important—not only for your company's leaders but for you in terms of your career, as well. We must all decide what we are going to do, moving forward. Are you going to operate from a position of fear and resist automation and technology, clinging to the belief that the predictions about how AI can assist us in the future are wrong? Or, are you going to embrace what is right around the next bend and jump onto the bandwagon early, to secure your position in a world that works with artificial intelligence?

As AI becomes more ensconced, and as more efficiencies are discovered and embraced, we all need to imagine how we can use it to make ourselves more productive and enhance our careers. We can all choose to be at the leading edge of a technology that can change our lives.

## ??? AIQ (Ask Intelligent Questions) ???

1. Look at your company and discover an operational area that can be improved with AI. Maybe it's an old, outdated internal process that currently relies on humans for work that could be automated (such as hiring or performance reviews), or something that was a challenging problem in the past that can be addressed using AI (such as outstanding receivables, drug reactions, or inventory). What used to be something "we have to tolerate because there is no easy solution" could be something that we can fix with AI.

2. Where can you start to create solutions through co-creation? Gather your team and brainstorm some solutions. Ask your team, "If X wasn't a problem, what would we look like now?" For instance: "If we didn't have to all come here to this office and work together, what would this meeting look like now?"

## People Plus Machines

Much of the scare-mongering that we hear about AI warns that thousands of jobs that will be lost. It focuses on unemployment and scarcity. We've been hearing the cry of "robots taking our jobs" since the dawn of the industrial revolution. It hasn't happened yet, so why are we expecting it to happen now?

Our future needs to be focused more on humans *plus* machines and not humans *or* machines. It doesn't have to be an either/or situation.

> Our future with AI needs to be
> focused more on *plus*, not *or*.

Our thinking needs to change from people versus machines to people plus machines. We can leverage AI to take care of a lot of the figurative heavy lifting involved in data crunching and management, and the actual heavy lifting such as cobots are currently doing on the factory lines.

As an example, in the future we will still need doctors. But working with AI, our doctors can do more, more efficiently. Currently, medical practitioners diagnose patients based on symptoms. That is something a machine can easily do. Computers currently have access to a patient's medical history and can determine whether a patient fits into a pattern characteristic of a specific disease. They can then make recommendations for treatment and suggest further tests. But that doesn't mean we would no longer have doctors. It's simply that their role would evolve. The doctor's primary role would change, to do what humans do best—relate to other humans. Doctors would take care of the relationship and conversations with patients. They can express empathy, understanding, and compassion in a way AI cannot. The doctor can explain what is happening, what to expect, and help to determine what the expectations of the patient are. They can listen to the patient's fears and validate their concerns. They can provide the emotional side of medicine that a machine simply cannot do.

The combination of "machine plus doctor" will prove to be more efficient and effective, in the same way that the combination of "machine plus teacher" will be. Machines will do the computing and technical aspects of many jobs, and humans, who are better able to see the bigger picture, will handle more human tasks like showing compassion and creating relationships. Those are skills and abilities that AI doesn't have at this point.

Keeping our eyes open to the possibilities of the future will be essential. We all need to adopt a new mindset that says that Alexa is not actually stealing your job, but instead making your job easier by offloading the time consuming, repetitive (and often boring) tasks that you do now. You will bring your personality, your compassion and your decision-making abilities to your job. Keep your eyes open to what you can offer that makes you unique.

## The Future of Work

Cheryl Cran is the founder of NextMapping™/NextMapping. com and the CEO of parent company Synthesis at Work Inc. In her white paper, Nextmapping™, Cran says we need to take the "opportunity to build our human skills such as empathy, emotional intelligence, collaborative skills, leadership skills, ability to inspire and influence, be more critical in (our) thinking, discern truth from fiction, and be more compassionate and loving."[60]

---

60  https://nextmapping.com/wp-content/uploads/2018/03/Whitepaper-If-Robots-are-the-Future-of-Work_What-s-Next-For-Humans.pdf

Companies and people should be preparing for the impact of AI in the workplace. We should expect job disruption—but not fear it. Our past has shown us that we will successfully navigate the changes that are coming. It doesn't mean it will be easy, but it does mean that we have done it in the past, and we can do it again in the future, and be better off in the long run.

> Our past has shown us that we will
> successfully navigate the changes.

Leaders need to be equipped so they can navigate the future of work. It is not just the tasks that are going to change; the way we lead is going to undergo a radical shift as well. Our leaders need to be able to not only anticipate where AI can benefit our companies, but be aware of the impact on workers and deal with that as well. They need compassion and understanding as well as decision-making skills and vision.

Leaders (and companies) today need to be agile and fast-acting so they can quickly change the way they do business as new ways are introduced. As employees, we need to be doing that, too. If we see that the company we are working for is exploring ways to integrate AI into our work processes, we should be among the first to jump on that bandwagon and learn as much about it as we possibly can.

Earlier, I provided the statistic from LinkedIn which showed a 190 per cent increase in AI skills from 2015 to 2017, according to the social media platform's Chief Data Officer, Igor Perisic. When asked what, exactly, "AI skills" are, Perisic explained that they are the skills needed to create artificial intelligence technologies such as neural networks, deep learning, and machine learning. Programming languages such as Weka and Scikit-Learn will soon be in much greater demand. "LinkedIn data shows all types of technical AI skills are growing at a rapid pace around the world," said Perisic.

Companies will need to build these capabilities either within the organization or externally, finding the new capabilities from an external source. They will need to ensure that they can work with them, adapt to them, and maximize what can be done with machine learning.

In the future, companies will require more knowledge workers. Companies need to focus on finding, attracting, and retaining high performing talent. To gain advantage over competitors, companies will be in a race to implement AI across all areas of operations.

Start paying attention to the race that is happening in your industry. Don't keep your head in the sand or hope that your industry isn't affected. Don't count the days until you can retire and hope that your job will last that long. Adapt. Learn. Grow.

If your company hasn't already started looking at AI solutions, have your competitors? Should you be looking?

The answer is *yes*. Yes, you should be looking at how AI can improve not only your efficiency, but your customer service. As an employee, you should be looking at improving your skills in the artificial intelligence arena as well.

The ideas presented in this book will certainly give you a good sense of what currently exists, and what you should be exploring to help you move your career or your company forward. Don't stop here. Continue to expand and explore areas in which your job can embrace AI. Look for ways to be the one at your workplace (or in your industry) to lead the charge to implement AI.

The jobs of the past aren't coming back. And that's a good thing, because we won't need them. We will be creating new ones that let machines do machine-work and allow humans to be the brains, the compassion and the expertise driving the new economy.

Find your place in the new workplace revolution. Embrace AI and the new technologies and opportunities that go along with it. Be where the future is—it's up to you!

## About the Author

Rhonda Scharf is a professional speaker, consultant, and author specializing in *people power*. She helps companies and individuals get on-the-right-track in terms of their productivity, efficiency, effectiveness and personal satisfaction. A well-recognized and respected speaker, trainer, and consultant in the field of administration, Rhonda is founder and CEO of ON THE RIGHT TRACK—Training & Consulting Inc. based in Ottawa, Ont. and Fort Myers, Fla.

In her more than 25 years with ON THE RIGHT TRACK, Rhonda has conducted more than 2,500 training sessions, workshops, and seminars—and has presented to tens of thousands of people worldwide. Her clients include Fortune 100 companies and beyond.

Rhonda's career in technology began at age 22, when she heard the phrase "*Help me, Rhonda!*" hundreds of times a day as she answered the help-desk line. Her career naturally transitioned into training, and she launched her own business in 1993.

Rhonda was inducted into the Canadian Speaking Hall of Fame, is a recipient of the Spirit of CAPS award, and earned her Certified Speaking Professional designation in 2002. She is currently only one of two speakers in the world to hold this trifecta of honors.

She has written seven other books focusing on administration, effectiveness, and efficiency in the workplace.

She is funny, thought-provoking, and happy to ask—and track down the answers for—the difficult questions.

9 781642 794014